Twayne's Filmmakers Series

Warren French
EDITOR

George Roy Hill

Credit: *Universal City Studios, Inc.*

George Roy Hill

EDWARD SHORES

BOSTON

Twayne Publishers

1983

George Roy Hill

is first published in 1983 by Twayne Publishers,
A Division of G. K. Hall & Company

Copyright © 1983 by G. K. Hall & Company

Printed on permanent/durable acid-free paper and bound
in the United States of America

First Printing, April 1983

175751

Library of Congress Cataloging in Publication Data

Shores, Edward.
  George Roy Hill.

  (Twayne's filmmakers series)
  Bibliography: p. 154
  Includes index.
  1. Hill, George Roy, 1922–   . I. Title.
  II. Series.
  PN1998.A3H487   791.43'0233'0924   82-6193
  ISBN 0-8057-9290-2   AACR2

Contents

About the Author

EDWARD SHORES was born in Binghamton, New York. He received his B.A. from the State University of New York at Binghamton in 1972. He received the Ph.D. in English from the University of Florida in 1977. His dissertation was on the films of George Roy Hill.

Editor's Foreword

OUR DECISION TO include a book about George Roy Hill in this auteurist-oriented series has raised more eyebrows than any other so far. While most of our consultants acknowledge the stylish polish of Hill's work, they tend to distrust his films as slick commercial productions with little depth that will make them long persist in the memory. Even the Academy Award sweep of *The Sting* is attributed to the public's longing for elegant escapist entertainment after a surfeit of sex and violence during a decade of "catastrophe films."

Publicity-shy Hill's refusal to make flamboyant demands for artistic autonomy and to far outstrip budgets in the pursuit of precise details needed to preserve his vision have put him—like Robert Aldrich—at a disadvantage in an era dominated by Francis Ford Coppola, Martin Scorsese, Steven Spielberg, and Michael Cimino, for example. Yet, although Hill has supplied the original source for only one of his major films, the interview he granted Edward Shores for use in the appendix to this book makes clear, though slowly and diffidently, that his films are not just isolated "assignments," but are informed by a common, consistent, pessimistic vision about the illusions of our culture. His major films are unified in ways that make them most impressive as a group, and a principal value of Shores's book is its implication that retrospectives of Hill's work might awaken viewers to a depth of thoughtful concern that has escaped attention.

Shores observes that another problem about Hill's work that may actually be one of its greatest sources of interest is a seeming lack of development. Instead of persisting in the perfection of a single genre in the manner of such traditional auteurs as John Ford, Alfred Hitchcock, and Cecil B. DeMille, Hill has moved in his seven most ambitious films so far from one genre to another—historical romance, musical comedy, Western, World War II tale, caper film, flying epic, and sports drama. (Curiously this group is bracketed by Hill's one admitted repetition of modest, low-keyed treatments of tentative young love affairs in *The World of Henry Orient* and *A Little Romance*.)

Shores concentrates on the last five of these spectacles, because of Hill's greater production control over them than over the popular *Hawaii* and *Thoroughly Modern Millie* that lack the coherence and concentration of their successors. Shores stresses the similarities of the visions underlying these experiments in several genres; but I think it may be possible to suggest an even further relationship between them that adds significantly to the importance of these films and Hill's work as a whole as landmarks in the evolution of American moviemaking.

In the introduction to *The South and Film* (1981), I argue, enlarging upon observations of many others, that

Since 1970 . . . it has been impossible to make credible films about the legendary West except parodies like Frank Perry's *Rancho Deluxe*, Howard Zieff's *Hearts of the West*, Robert Altman's *Buffalo Bill and the Indians*, and Mel Brooks's *Blazing Saddles*. (An attempt in the summers of 1979 and 1980 with films like *Butch and Sundance: The Early Years* and *The Long Riders* has only made the truth of this observation embarrassingly apparent. The Old West of the films had been shot down with Butch Cassidy and the Sundance Kid in 1969.)

After reading Shores's manuscript, I got to thinking about George Roy Hill's four pictures following his valedictory to the prevailing myth of the Old West, and it struck me that parallel observations could also be made that they "shot down" the genres that they brought to spectacular culminations. No World War II film has been a success since George C. Scott starred in *Patton* (1970), and the Kurt Vonnegut/George Roy Hill *Slaughterhouse-Five* deglamorizes the events celebrated in such epics as *The Longest Day* in the same ironic manner that *Butch Cassidy* . . . did the dramatic posturings of Western outlaws.

Shores finds *irony* "a major tool" in Hill's work; and the successful imposition of an ironic vision on a romantic genre usually indicates the loss of the magical power of its earlier naive narratives. Certainly such a fate overtook the "caper" films like *How to Steal a Million* and *Charade* that had increasingly trivialized the excruciating tensions induced by Jules Dassin's *Rififi* (1956) and *Topkapi* (1964). After the distancing achieved by the magazine-illustration set-pieces and then exotic music in *The Sting* rendered the con man's world as much a remote fantasy as Butch Cassidy's vanished West, no one attempted a sequel, because any repetition would have seemed even "phonier" than the schemes depicted. The downbeat ending spelled *finis* rather than suggesting more to come.

The Great Waldo Pepper and *Slapshot* may seem, on superficial inspection, to invalidate my point, since, despite their ironies, they do not seem the end of any generic trail. While I was reading Shores's manuscript, however, I happened across Stuart Byron's remarks in the *Village Voice* about "the near-total demise of the big-budget genres which had sustained Hollywood since talkies began."[1] These Byron defined as "the western, the war film, the musical, the thriller, the comedy of manners, the gangster film." What this familiar list brings to mind is that neither the airplane film nor the sports film had ever developed into a major genre—despite efforts to promote them. The airplane film did start off well when it was associated with World War I in *Wings* and *The Dawn Patrol*, but later efforts to broaden the genre like Howard Hawks's *Only Angels Have Wings* (1939) and Douglas Sirk's *The Tarnished Angels* (1958) failed to establish it. Despite this nation's addiction to sports, the sport film never really caught on despite attempts from *The Pride of the Yankees* (1942) to *Paper Lion* (1968). The reason for the failure of these two genres is too complicated to go into here, but is surely a problem worth the speculation of historians of popular taste.

Even so, it is conspicuous that, since Hill's films, there have been no successful ones in either genre, except heavily ironic ones like *North Dallas Forty*. He was dealing again with romantic material as doomed as that employed in the earlier films; and very likely generic rather than individual problems are responsible for *The Great Waldo Pepper* and *Slapshot* being less successful than the three earlier ones.

What this simplified account is meant to suggest is that Hill has played, however unintentionally, an extraordinary kind of "killer" role, taking the genres that have principally sustained Hollywood through its years of intellectual innocence and giving their characteristically upbeat fables, just at the moment that they had reached the end of their ropes, ironic, downbeat twists in stylish productions that truly "froze" the actions. It is not surprising that such films appeared when they did; but it is surprising that they are all the work of one man. (*Thoroughly Modern Millie* even came close to having the same relationship to the musical, but it lacked the "sting" of *Cabaret* and *New York, New York*.) As an artist whose work represents the end of an age, Hill is a figure that film historians are going to have to reckon with.

As this book goes to press, Hill's future is inscrutable. *Slapshot* appears to have ended a phase of his work. On the basis of the novel

GEORGE ROY HILL

from which it derives, *The World According to Garp* seems unlikely to have any relationship to traditional film genres. Having nailed old coffins shut, will Hill be able—as author John Irving seemingly has been in the novel—to give birth to profitable new film genres? Shores's book comes just at a time when it may help us to understand the preliminary work of an artist on the verge of an even more significant phase of his career.

W. F.

Preface

COMMERCIAL FILM is the forbidden zone for most film critics. The products of the entertainment industry are so easily explained in terms of old formulas that it seems even newspaper reviewers can adequately assess them; the critic's touch is reserved for those films which enlarge our understanding of the medium and the world. On the whole such a distinction seems valid. The blatantly mercenary aims of many Hollywood epics are clear from stories in the trade presses: producers announce their intentions to capitalize on news events; stars are hired for their box-office potential; scripts are rewritten to appeal to the lowest common denominator. When popular films draw attention it is often as evidence to support some nonfilmic view. Michael Cimino's *The Deer Hunter,* for example, an enormously popular film, was reviewed in film journals, but the major issues were its politics, or its social and cultural significance, not its aesthetic properties. The critics' concern with mainstream directors is almost always in direct proportion to their independence from the traditional entertainment vehicle; it is the breaking of the mold, the attempt to go beyond the ordinary that is encouraged and discussed. But even the most reliable of generalizations has its exceptions, and the compartmentalizing of cinema into "worthwhile" and "escapist" categories can lead one to overlook films of merit. Such is the case, I believe, with the work of George Roy Hill.

I originally saw most of Hill's films because they were labeled entertainments, additions to the student's diet of works by artists like Fellini, Antonioni, Bergman. The films, however, did not comfortably fit into the escapist category. They were entertaining—superb examples of narrative filmmaking—but there was an ambiguity to them, a divergence from the expected genre formulas that set them apart from more ordinary fare. These variations were more than twists to keep the audience's interest; they seemed part of a conscious attempt to go beyond the calculation and pandering overt in many genre examples. I found that, should I leave my preconceptions behind, Hill's films worked on levels other than that of the narrative. There was an intelligent, questioning mind behind these films, a craftsman who could use a shot to advance a story and simultaneously fashion a commentary on the subject. This commentary, once perceived, took the form of a critical questioning of the traditional themes inherent in the genres Hill had chosen. In addition to the entertainment promised, I found myself watching films which subtly examined the conventions they superficially endorsed.

Hill's films became interesting not only for the aesthetic pleasure provided, but also because of their focus. He dealt with the essences of American culture: the idea of individuality, the drive for success, the myth of the happy family, the effect of our expansion westward on our collective imagination. Moreover, the enormous success of his films (at one time Hill had two of Hollywood's ten all-time moneymakers) suggested that the concepts depicted in his films closely matched those of the filmgoing public. The ironic treatment of these themes essentially subverted the passive, complacent understanding encouraged by the traditional genre narratives. Individualism was no longer the single, viable option for the American; families turned out to be sources of trouble as well as refuges; and success became a burden, the achievement of it a limitation rather than a reward. Such criticism, of course, had been ventured before, but Hill's films were distinct in several ways. They were not message oriented; no hero stopped to summarize the moral or utter edifying homilies about the community or the need for spiritual goals. The films were not directed to that minority of viewers who can respond to a complex, unconventional work. Finally, the criticism in them is not pat or predictable. Hill's films may show the weaknesses of individuality or the family, but at the same time there is a genuine appreciation of these concepts, an understanding that there was once much of value contained in them. A tension exists between the conventional perceptions of the world and Hill's criticism that prevents the easy, cynical dismissal of them. More than anything else, Hill's films encourage us to think about a culture often accepted without examination.

For a number of reasons, his own desire for personal privacy among them, Hill remains one of the more obscure American directors; his films receive praise for the skill of execution, but few people take them or their thematic concerns seriously. This study attempts to rectify that situation by examining in detail his six most recent films—*Butch Cassidy and the Sundance Kid, Slaughterhouse-Five, The Sting, The Great Waldo Pepper, Slapshot,* and *A Little Romance*—that are Hill's best work. The five early films are not included, not only because (with the exception of *The World of Henry Orient*) they lack the maturity of the later films, but because their inclusion would only extend, not alter the basic points of this study.

Each reading shows how Hill controls the film to develop specific themes, using traditional film elements to create works which encompass more than their nominal subjects. As a group, the readings suggest some of the ideas that have absorbed Hill throughout his career and the ways in which his views have developed over time. The goal is not only to illuminate the strengths and virtues of the individual works, but to focus attention on an artist whose past achievements and continued growth deserve more than our casual glances.

In addition, the book concludes with an interview in which George Roy Hill discusses his films with this author.

Edward Shores

Chronology

1922	George Roy Hill born on December 20 to George R. and Helen Frances (Owens) Hill.
1943	B.A. from Yale University. Studies music.
1943–1945	Serves in Marine Corps as a transport plane pilot.
1946–1949	Studies music and literature at Trinity College in Dublin. Receives a B. Litt in 1949. Makes acting debut with Cyril Cusack at the Abbey Theatre.
1953	*My Brother's Keeper*, first teleplay, presented on the *Kraft Television Theater*.
1956	Produces, directs, and co-authors the teleplay *A Night to Remember* (presented on the *Kraft Television Theater*). Receives two Emmy award nominations, one for directing and one for writing.
1957	Directs *The Helen Morgan Story* (presented on CBS *Playhouse 90*); receives an Emmy award nomination. Directs first Broadway play, Ketti Fring's adaptation of Thomas Wolfe's *Look Homeward, Angel*.
1958	Directs *Child of Our Time* (presented on CBS *Playhouse 90*). Receives Emmy award nomination.
1959	Directs *Judgment at Nuremburg* for CBS *Playhouse 90*. Directs *The Gang's All Here*, a play about Warren Harding.
1960	Directs Tennessee Williams's *Period of Adjustment*.
1962	Directs first film, the adaptation of *Period of Adjustment*.
1963	*Toys in the Attic*.
1964	*The World of Henry Orient*.
1966	*Hawaii*.
1967	*Henry, Sweet Henry*, a musical based on *The World of Henry Orient*, has a brief run on Broadway; Hill's last

appearance as a theater director. *Thoroughly Modern Millie*.

1969   *Butch Cassidy and the Sundance Kid*. Receives nomination for an Academy Award for best director.

1972   *Slaughterhouse-Five*.

1973   *The Sting*. Wins Academy Award for best director; *The Sting* receives six other awards, including best picture.

1975   *The Great Waldo Pepper*.

1977   *Slapshot*.

1979   *A Little Romance*.

1

A Survey of the Films

GEORGE ROY HILL has never been accorded the status given to such older American directors as John Ford, Frank Capra, Raoul Walsh, or Howard Hawks, nor is he ranked with such current luminaries as Francis Coppola, Martin Scorsese, Robert Altman, or Arthur Penn. Such a judgment, however, is neither final nor accurate. As this study will attempt to show, Hill deserves consideration as an American film artist, for his work is a careful meditation on the American culture, an intelligent, continuing exploration of it that ranks with the best contemporary work. The overtly commercial surface of his work masks, but does not obliterate, the intelligence of his films, and his commercial success is a mark of his skill, not his mediocrity. He controls the elements of film to create works that are simultaneously entertaining and serious, and this study will explore the way in which Hill works and the central thematic concerns of his films.

Perhaps one reason Hill is overlooked is that his career as a director seems an afterthought to his work in television and the stage. He did not direct a film until he was forty, and did not commit himself full time to films until 1967. He was not an avid filmgoer as a youngster, and he does not evidence that obsession with and comprehensive knowledge of films that often marks younger directors. Yet Hill's emergence as a first-rate director is not accidental; it is the natural result of his lifelong interest in the arts, a discovery that the medium of film offered opportunities amenable to his particular creative skills.

Hill started as a music student at Yale University. While there he participated in the Glee Club, was a member of the Whiffenpoof Society, and headed the Yale Dramat. After graduation in 1943, he

1

The madcap trio from Thoroughly Modern Millie *(left to right)*
Mary Tyler Moore, Julie Andrews, Carol Channing.
(Credit: Movie Star News)

entered the Marine Corps as a pilot and served in the Pacific Theater. Later, following the war, he studied music and literature at Trinity College in Dublin, Ireland, and acting with Cyril Cusack at the Abbey Theater. Although Hill took a B. Litt from Trinity College, acting won out over literature and he returned to New York to make his living in that profession. While Hill was able to work as an actor, he never achieved any great success. Instead Hill, a very private person, eventually found that the stress felt before a performance no longer outweighed the satisfaction of performing. As he approached his thirtieth birthday, Hill, like many others, was struggling to establish and distinguish himself in his chosen field.

The Korean War interrupted that struggle, for Hill was recalled to active duty and spent eighteen months at the Marine Corps jet-pilot training center at Cherry Point, North Carolina. Since off-duty recreational activities were scarcer, Hill began writing in his spare time. He sold his first teleplay, *My Brother's Keeper*, to the *Kraft Television Theater* in 1953, and after his discharge returned to New York to work as a writer and a director. The shift from in front of to behind the camera was the proverbial turning point, the discovery of a vocation that called forth all of his creative energies and opened new worlds of exploration. Within a short time Hill established himself as one of television's leading producer/writer/directors. In 1956 he was nominated for two Emmy awards (for writing and direction) for *A Night to Remember,* one of the most complex live television dramas ever presented. He was also responsible for *The Helen Morgan Story* (1957), the original *Judgment at Nuremburg* (1959), and over fifty dramas in television's golden age.

Yet television changed as the networks discovered the financial benefits of series, and the opportunities to do meaningful work were reduced. Like other television directors (Arthur Penn, Sidney Lumet, and Franklin Schaffner), Hill searched for other media which offered him the kind of material and the degree of control he needed to work effectively. Theater was Hill's first new world, and in 1957 he directed his first play, an adaptation of Thomas Wolfe's *Look Homeward, Angel.* He also received several offers to direct films, but he turned most of these down. Only two projects ever reached the preparatory stage, and both of these fell through. It was not until he was offered the opportunity to direct *Period of Adjustment* (from the Tennessee Williams play that he had directed on Broadway) that Hill was able to make the leap to film.

A second reason that he remains relatively unknown is that an overview of his film career tends to support the prevailing critical judgment. Hill began with two play adaptations, *Period of Adjustment* (1962) and Lillian Hellman's *Toys in the Attic* (1963), which, though fairly well received, were not indicative of great cinematic virtuosity. *Period of Adjustment* is essentially a filmed play. The camera is almost always at middle distance, providing a frame like the proscenium arch. The actors move about the frame the way they would on a stage, establishing character and ideas through position and dialogue. There is little camera movement, few close-ups, and only functional lighting. *Toys in the Attic* is a step forward cinematically, for the camera begins to move, the close-up is discovered, and the lighting helps convey ideas and character. Hill uses the camera to tell the story instead of relying on the conventions of the stage. But in two of his next three films, *Hawaii* (1966) and *Thoroughly Modern Millie* (1967), there is little evidence of further growth; the camera is only a functional, recording device. *Hawaii* is a picture-postcard film, with the action framed and presented in the traditional Hollywood cinematic grammar; *Thoroughly Modern Millie* is similar with well-lit sets and straightforward camera use. Only *The World of Henry Orient* (1964) received widespread approval, garnering praise for its unusual story, the fresh performances Hill evoked from the teenage actresses, and its skillful cinematic presentation of adolescence.

Thematically, his work also seems conventional. The themes of the plays and *Hawaii* were set by the original sources, and Hill, while perhaps altering them slightly for public consumption, did not change them in any significant fashion. *The World of Henry Orient* concerns a young girl's growth to maturity, and *Thoroughly Modern Millie* is solely an entertainment. Hill's work with the thematic concerns of others was competent, a translation to the screen, not a new creation that incorporated the essence of the old. Of his two original works, *The World of Henry Orient* seems the innovative retelling of a traditional theme rather than the breaking of new ground by an original talent.

However, in these early films, particularly in *Henry Orient*, subjects and themes are similar to, though not as fully realized as, those in the later films, and a clear continuity of interest is evident. Even though Hill's early films came primarily from other media, he nonetheless selected projects which suited his point of view. Julian Berniers, for example, the male protagonist of *Toys in the Attic*, is

Max Von Sydow as Abner Hale and his son, Clas, as Micha Hale, in Hawaii.
(Credit: Movie Star News)

similar to the protagonists in all Hill's films in that he is an outsider
and a dreamer. Marked by his repeated failure in life, and his marriage to a child-woman, Julian longs to overturn his black sheep status
through a deal that will enrich and redeem him. His sister, Carrie, set
apart by her spinsterhood, is a dreamer of a more obsessive nature.
She clings to the suffocating, failed brother–possessive sister relationship of the past, attempting to keep it intact, with a warped
intensity that is nearly fatal. Eventually her manipulations are successful, but Julian, though again a failure, sees her treachery, accepts
responsibility for his own actions, and leaves her behind. Carrie is
destroyed by her devotion to her dream, while Julian is saved because he realizes the harmful nature of his fantasies.

The Reverend Hale of *Hawaii* is another outsider, distinguished
even among missionaries for his puritanical zeal. The world he envi-
sions, and struggles so diligently to realize, is a Christian paradise
which redeems the lost Hawaiians. Yet, like Julian and Carrie Berniers, his narrow-minded devotion to his ideal blinds him to the
actuality of his situation and leads to personal suffering and social

disaster. When the dream is shattered, the Reverend Hale is almost destroyed with it, but he is rescued by his discovery of a new, more humane Christianity. Once again the failed dreamer is reprieved by discovery of a new set of values.

A second interesting feature of *Hawaii* is its treatment of the American experience. It deals specifically with the development and extension of our culture's values, showing a darkness most commercial films gloss over. While this examination of our expansion in *Hawaii* is too clear, almost didactic, Hill will later tackle other aspects of American culture—sports, war, the West—with more subtlety and thoroughness.

The World of Henry Orient is a comic variant of the dreamer story. Both Val Boyd and Marian Gilbert are distinct from typical adolescents by virtue of their intelligence and sensitivity. Unable to fit in the small world of their girls' school, Val and Gil seek romance and adventure, as suggested by their romp in Central Park and their fantasies of pirates. They eventually formulate a fantasy—that of the great lover, Henry Orient—when Val develops a crush on the inept pianist. The complications as they try to mine this fantasy and discover the nuances of Henry's life produce some comic moments, even though it is apparent that Val's dream will certainly collapse. We can see that Henry is a poseur, a putative seducer whose character is as shallow as his playing is tortured. The obvious thrust of the plot is complicated by the return of Val's parents, and the unhappiness of her family life puts her dreaming into a new perspective. She fantasizes because there is so little left for her to believe in at home, and, unable to agree with her suspicious mother and her ineffective father, she places all her hopes of happiness with Henry Orient. The discovery of his falseness is thus more painful than the collapse of an adolescent fantasy since Val has invested so much of herself into the dream. She runs away from home, disillusioned and bitter. Yet Val is also saved because her father finally reasserts himself, boots out the unfaithful wife, and recommits himself to family values. Once again the broken dreamer is saved by the discovery of more enduring values.

The quest to fulfill a dream remains a part of all Hill's films, and it is later refined from a simple narrative vehicle into the representative American experience, the key that allows Hill to explore our society. He alters the quest story by taking away the traditional refuge of commercial cinema, that fortuitous rediscovery of the verities (family, Christian values) of our culture, and is thus able to develop more

Tense trios: (top) Jane Fonda surrounded by glowering Tony Franciosa and watchful Jim Hutton in Period of Adjustment: *(bottom) Peter Sellers surrounded by Tippy Walker and Merrie Spaeth (right) in* The World of Henry Orient. *(Courtesy: Museum of Modern Art/Film Stills Archive)*

complex and searching studies of the familiar America found in Hollywood films. The ambiguous endings which characterize his later films reflect not only a growing pessimism, but also a growing artistic sensibility that is no longer satisfied with the conventional boundaries of film.

After these first five films, however, Hill remained virtually unknown. In the increasingly film-conscious world of the 1960s, Hill's efforts seemed part of an outdated commercial tradition. He went to successes from the stage or novel, or tried-and-true genre formulas, to guarantee himself an audience, and appeared to lack an intrinsic interest in film as an aesthetic phenomenon. New directors, on the other hand, were becoming more conscious of the film tradition, and using and commenting on it in their works. They were concerned with style, experiential reality, studies of the human spirit, or creating their own unique world.[1] Critical acclaim went to the imaginative explorations of Antonioni, Fellini, Bergman, and the New Wave of French directors; American directors like Siegel and Bogdanovitch were touted, early directors rediscovered, critical theory was pushed in new directions, and politics was made a criteria of film excellence. Commercial films like Hill's seemed to belong to an appreciated, but no longer relevant past.

In 1969, Hill released *Butch Cassidy and the Sundance Kid,* an enormously popular and successful Western that seemed proof of Hill's commercial craftsmanship and conventionality. His subsequent efforts, *Slaughterhouse-Five* (1972), *The Sting* (1973), *The Great Waldo Pepper* (1975), *Slapshot* (1977), and *A Little Romance* (1979) all received similar critical treatment: perfunctory acknowledgment of the craftsmanship and an occasional sigh that such efforts were being put into commercial exploitation. The more serious of the American popular reviewers—Pauline Kael, John Simon, Stanley Kaufmann, Andrew Sarris—praised overt attempts to use the medium to aesthetic ends. Robert Altman's experiments with genre and the elements of narrative and sound, Arthur Penn's thematic concerns, Martin Scorsese's ventures into the underside of America or into Hollywood genres, Francis Coppola's powerful narrative vision—these received critical approbation. Hill's position as a talented, "studio" type director seemed fixed, and he is currently relegated to the status of Herbert Ross, Arthur Hiller, or older studio reliables like Mervyn LeRoy or Michael Curtiz.

Most European critics avoid comment on Hill's work, but it is doubtful, considering its commercialism, that many would be interested. Unconcerned with film history or film form, still centered on the individual, avoiding political issues, ignoring the place of cinema in the revolutionary class struggle,[2] Hill's films must seem unimaginative exercises in commercialism rather than the work of an artist who rises above the restrictions of the Hollywood entertainment system. In fact, Hill's films possess none of the great virtues of all revolutionary films—narrative intransitivity, estrangement, foregrounding, multiple digesis, unpleasure, and reality—enumerated by Peter Wollen.[3] These movies are straightforward, entertaining, and comprehensible examples of the "reactionary bourgeois capitalist cinema."

This study attempts to revise the prevailing critical opinion of Hill by showing that his control of form and content and his use of the medium rank him among the best of America's directors. Instead of imitating past conventions, as he is often accused of doing, Hill manipulates them to create his own unique form, a controlled ironic fable that dissects the very conventions it supposedly endorses. Instead of rehashing accepted wisdom or the impoverished dicta of an earlier era, Hill offers his own understanding: he attempts to create the world anew, as every artist must, to make it comprehensible for the viewer. His work evidences the critical intelligence, the craftsmanship, and the intuitive understanding that mark the efforts of any conscious artist. Whether or not Hill's judgments and understanding will stand the test of time remains to be seen, but his best work is an intelligent cinematic exploration of the American experience.

Hill's films can be seen as a continuing critique of the ideas which have shaped and still support the American culture. He questions such traditional concepts as the nobility of individual heroism, the role and nature of the family, and the American obsession with success. These concepts are a small part of a core of ideas that can be termed "conventional morality," wisdom that, whatever its origins, comes to be accepted as given by the members of a culture. The configuration of this morality is ambiguous, but a suggestive and subjective outline can be drawn. The conventional wisdom with which Hill's films deal holds that the forces of good invariably triumph over the forces of evil; that righteousness is rewarded while wrongdoing is punished; that the universe is providentially and benevolently ruled; that the family is a strong force for good; that violence, if channeled in socially approved directions, is acceptable; that union with society is a person's most important goal; that the development of the individual spirit is a person's most important goal; that acts of heroism are meaningful and add to a person's stature; that marriage is the ideal relationship between two people; that success marks the individual; and that material success is secondary to emotional happiness. The list could be extended, but this at least suggests what is meant by conventional morality.[4]

Of course, these ideas have been attacked by filmmakers from the 1930s on. More recently, Arthur Penn's *Bonnie and Clyde* and Sam Peckinpah's *The Wild Bunch* both exploded traditional concepts of violence by revealing the gore which previous Hollywood films had glossed over. Films about failures, such as Bob Rafelson's *Five Easy Pieces,* or unconventional heroes, such as William Friedkin's *The French Connection*, reaped financial success, and films that concentrated on the seamier side of life were no longer taboo. *Midnight Cowboy* dealt with a derelict and a male prostitute; *Klute* had a female prostitute as a heroine; and *Easy Rider* focused on two drug dealers. Directors began to play with conventions, using them to other ends than those for which they were originally intended. Roman Polanski's *Chinatown* both parallels and departs from the conventions of the detective thriller, and suggests a decidedly different understanding of evil than that found in most private-eye films. Robert Altman's *McCabe and Mrs. Miller* and Arthur Penn's *The Missouri Breaks* both show an underside of the American experience that was never captured in the traditional Western films which theirs recall.

Despite the proliferation of such efforts and a general shift in attitude away from the optimism of the thirties, the postwar hope of the forties, and the television world of the fifties, the traditional film and the conventional morality remain firmly entrenched. The cultural unity that permitted the development of the Hollywood entertainments may no longer exist, but the conventional narratives and morality still exert a great attraction for the majority of Americans. Walt Disney's efforts still meet with considerable success, and "traditional" stories, if done well, can expect to reap a profit. *The Sound of Music, Mary Poppins, A Star is Born* (1977), *Jaws, The Other Side of the Mountain*, and *Rocky* have all done well with the public despite their lack of innovation or great artistry. The industry's greatest success, *Star Wars,* seems a hit precisely because it captures the optimism, enthusiasm, and simplicity of an earlier era.

Hill, like Altman, Penn, and Polanski, challenges these still prevailing concepts of conventional morality. His films tell us that these trusted ideas are antiquated; the simple truths they espouse are inconsistent with the more complex modern world. Identification with and acceptance of the concepts does not bring happiness, for an orderly and comprehensible world does not exist. For Hill, these concepts are lenses that distort perception and lead the individual into limiting, enervating, and occasionally self-destructive actions. In contrast, Hill presents a world where ambiguity, not clarity, is quintessential and where happiness is not inevitable. He disavows or dispassionately examines the cultural conventions, asking that we understand as well as accept them, and, if necessary, reject them. He calls, in essence, for a new independence, a personal determination of one's attitudes, aims, and understanding. His films, like those of most critically acclaimed new directors, stand as a challenge to the old ways of seeing and defining self.

Hill's films contravert conventional thought through *irony*. He weaves variations on the stereotypical characters and plots in with the conventional action to give his stories more substance and depth. The contrast between the familiar genre story and the variations creates an ambiguity that prevents the easy identification common to most genre films. Hill emotionally distances the audience from the characters, and makes possible a critical evaluation of them and their actions.

Each Hill film has two stories: (1) a genre story, and (2) an exploration of the genre story, its characters, plot, and metaphysics, much as Godard's *Breathless* is, in James Monaco's words, "at one and the same time a Gangster story and an essay about Gangster films."[5] The first stands as a frame of reference which allows us to evaluate and understand the variable second, and a perception of their relationship yields an understanding greater than that yielded by either of the parts. As Leo Braudy says, "genre in films can be the equivalent of conscious reference to tradition in the other arts." The use and variation of conventions is one way the artist can get at the metaphysics of a traditional form. Braudy writes that "the possibility exists in all art that convention and comment coexist, that overlapping and even contradictory assumptions and conventions may be brought into play to test their power and make the audience reflect on why they were assumed."[6]

The process is instantaneous, hardly as prolonged as the description, as a few examples will show. In Mel Brooks's *Blazing Saddles* the cowboys solemnly gather around the campfire to eat beans, a scene immediately reminiscent of many in earlier Western films. When the cowboys suffer from gas, the audience laughs, not only because the bathroom humor appeals to many, but also because the second scene is a witty variation of the genre scene. The two are essentially juxtaposed for us, and the contiguity yields an additional humor. We realize that the earlier Hollywood scene was unrealistic in its glossing over of natural body functions, and we laugh because the exaggerated variation ridicules the unwarranted modesty. In Robert Altman's *M*A*S*H*, the hospital scenes are much more realistic than those found in most Hollywood war films. The conventional, antiseptic pain of the earlier films serves as a point of reference, and the contrast between the two reveals the essential falsity of the Hollywood treatment of war. The characters function in the same way. Hawkeye and Trapper John, despite their self-interest and lack of overt courage, seem much more realistic and human than, say, the John Wayne character in *Back to Bataan*.

In addition, films are occasionally less obvious in their manipulation of genre conventions. Leo Braudy notes that:

The genre film lures its audience into a seemingly familiar world, filled with reassuring stereotypes of character, action, and plot. But the world may actually not be so lulling, and, in some cases, acquiescence in convention will turn out to be bad judgment or even a moral flaw—the basic theme of such Hitchcock films as *Blackmail* (1929), *Rear Window* (1954), and *Psycho*. . . . The very relaxing of the critical intelligence of the audience, the relief that we need not make decisions—aesthetic, moral, metaphysical—about the film, allows the genre film to use our expectations against themselves, and, in the process, reveal to us expectations and assumptions that we may never have thought we had.[7]

Altman's *McCabe and Mrs. Miller,* Hal Ashby's *Shampoo*, and John Schlesinger's *Darling* all work in this manner. I would contend that Hill's films work the same way: perception of the alternate story comes only through careful attention to detail, and understanding only when we see the complex relationship between original and variation. In order to show how Hill's films work, I shall first sketch in the variations of the standard story that prevent complete identification with the characters, then broadly outline the elements of Hill's alternate story, and finally draw some conclusions from an examination of the two.

All Hill's works belong to the category of commercial movies, films which, despite their variety, have remarkably similar characters, structures, and morality. In these films, representative characters resolve problems or achieve happiness by voluntarily accepting and practicing the tenets of conventional morality. The characters may begin outside society, such as Harry Morgan in Hawks's *To Have and Have Not,* the iconoclastic Fred Astaire figure in the musical comedies, or the classic Western hero, such as Tom Donaphon in *The Man Who Shot Liberty Valence,* and then move to a reconciliation with society, or remain outside society but essentially endorse its values. Or the character may begin as a member of society and then reaffirm its power by using its values and resources to defeat an enemy. Whatever the case, the characters usually move through a series of trials, eventually finding happiness through acceptance of conventional morality. The films thus become implicit or explicit advocates of the American culture; entertainments, but nonetheless assertions of the fundamental validity of certain values.

Although Hill's films seem produced from this mold, they are more accurately variations of it. Ideally, and this is true in such recent commercial ventures as *Rocky, Jaws, The Exorcist,* and *Star Wars,* the central characters, no matter what their limitations, ultimately embody a number of virtues with which the audience can identify and toward which it can feel sympathetic. Loyalty, courage, integrity, friendship, moral character are emphasized or, more often, emerge as the character undergoes a series of trials: town drunks reform, failures succeed, refugees from love become romantic, uncommitted figures turn patriotic, cowards gain courage, and sinners repent. The protagonists draw us into the world of the film, allowing us to experience vicariously the emotions around which the film is structured, and tacitly teaching us the moral lessons of our culture. Hill's characters, like all genre figures, have attractive qualities which draw us to them, and their problems—conflict with an increasingly bureaucratic or technological world, or a dispirited or materialistic one—engage our sympathy. But complicating the familiar frame are flaws that prevent total identification. Eventually the protagonists demonstrate some weakness, insensitivity, or failing that negates their hold on our feelings, drawing instead our wonder or disapprobation. We begin to question the characters, and in that questioning move away from the unthinking stock response. In addition, these flaws, unlike those of traditional characters, are never truly overcome; they stay with the characters throughout and, by virtue of their presence, contribute to our sense of ambiguity. The weaknesses are sometimes well-hidden, as in *The Sting,* or obvious, as in *Waldo Pepper,* but are always an integral part of the film.

A *menacing Beatrice Lille enjoys a social moment with Mary Tyler Moore, Julie Andrews and James Fox in* Thoroughly Modern Millie.
(Courtesy: Museum of Modern Art/Film Stills Archive)

The outlaw heroes of *Butch Cassidy* are lovable, charming, attractive figures whose stereotypical strengths are counterpointed by their seemingly limitless capacity for bad judgment. As the film progresses, their inability to see the hopelessness of their situation becomes a mark of their limitation, not their charm. Any sympathetic judgment is qualified by recognition that their independence is as much stumbled into as chosen; they do not understand the consequences of their actions. They contrast dramatically to the characters in *The Wild Bunch*, who *decide* to adhere to their old values rather than submit to the new technological world. Before the climactic shootout, Pike and Dutch exchange glances, indicating that they know the probable outcome of returning for Angel, but accept those consequences of their actions.

Billy Pilgrim is an engaging, but impotent naif who accepts prisons, such as life in Ilium, with a perseverance that borders on masochism. He lacks the ability or initiative to solve his problems, and accordingly his "triumph" on Trafamadore is more accidental and fantastic than earned. Despite our sympathy for him, he never becomes competent or strong enough to draw our identification. Hooker and Gondorff are roguishly charming con men, but no charm can hide the fact that "the sting" is performed as much for self-gratification as for revenge. At the end of the film, they deny that justice, the motive that has sanctioned their actions and made them more sympathetic than Lonnegan, is attainable or even worthwhile. This last minute reversal mutes some of our strong feelings for them and negates an unthinking emotional response to them.

While Waldo Pepper emerges victorious over Kessler, his road to that victory seems accidental, not earned. In addition, his lie about the fight with Kessler, his inability to learn from the experiences of his friends, and his failure in the attempted rescue of Mary Beth are qualities inconsistent with those usually associated with heroes. Once again the complete identification customary in commercial film is lacking. Reggie Dunlop of *Slapshot* demonstrates few of the virtues we expect to find in a conventional protagonist. There is no sensitivity or understanding hidden beneath his rough exterior; the crudity is the man. The championship cannot disguise the fact that Dunlop has manipulated the emotions of his players, ruined his own marriage, and almost destroyed the neurotic Lily Braden.

Daniel and Lauren, the teenage protagonists of *A Little Romance*, are among Hill's most engaging characters. They have a sensitivity and an ingenuous love that sharply contrasts to their parents' world. Yet they are also dominated by cultural ideas about romance, particuarly Daniel, who attempts to fulfill the ideal of manhood that he sees set forth in films. By paying such close attention to that concept, he comes close to losing Lauren.

The variations in character, which suggest an additional dimension to the films, are adumbrated and buttressed by the variations in structure. In conventional films, the character moves from a state of tension or estrangement to one of harmony and order through acquiesence to the conventional morality. Whatever problems the characters encounter are eventually resolved by an appeal to the precepts of traditional widsdom. They (and we) learn the "proper" way to act and think, and the world becomes clearer and less threatening. In John Ford's *The Man Who Shot Liberty Valence*, for example, Ransom Stoddard, and the civilization which he both endorses and represents, is threatened by the anarchic violence of Liberty Valence. Stoddard refuses to use force, attempting instead to break Valence's hold through the law, education, and the press. When that fails, he eventually learns that socially approved violence is occasionally necessary to establish and defend society. It is also carefully marked as a precondition to civilization, for we can see that those who practice violence, like Tom Donaphon, despite the honor and respect accorded them, are by their very nature excluded from society. Other Western films, like George Stevens's *Shane*, preach the same concepts, as did almost all Hollywood war films. Gangster films almost always begin with the criminals in the ascendency, move through periods of greater criminal success, and usually end with the criminal a victim of his own arrogance or other failings and the law victorious because of its superior intelligence or moral strength. Evil, it seems, contributes to its own destruction, while the law is by its nature triumphant. Whether or not crime is actually that simple is beside the point; the movies usually portrayed it in that manner. Romantic films usually involved some separation of the lovers, or some basic misunderstanding, as in *Top Hat*, that had to be overcome before the happy conclusion of marriage. Films like *Mildred Pierce*, *Imitation of Life* and *Young Man with a Horn* depicted people attempting to achieve success. Those characters usually reached their goal, but lost the much more valuable spiritual wealth of family and friends that has almost always been endorsed in popular culture. At the end, they usually recognized this commonplace of conventional wisdom and learned a bitter lesson, or else were reprieved and given another chance. The variations of the commercial story are endless, but the basic structure remains the same: those who accept conventional morality gain happiness.

In Hill's films, this basic structure is reversed. The characters have problems *because they accept the dictates of conventional wisdom*, not because they have cut themselves off from it. They begin as firm adherents to some quintessentially American belief and untypically move to a state of estrangement or tension because of their adherence to that belief. Such a basic reversal of structure alters the thematic thrust of Hill's films. Conventional morality hinders, not aids the comprehension of the world, and consequently, its validity is undercut.

In *Butch Cassidy,* for example, the outlaws are prime examples of American individuality. They reject the closed technological society and insist on their right to lead their own lives. Ordinarily such an attitude would be supported or shown as a source of strength, but Hill shows their blind adherence as a weakness leading to death. Their inability to see that the concept of unfettered individualism is no longer valid destroys them. Waldo Pepper and Reggie Dunlop are

typically American in their pursuit of excellence and success. Identification with them is easy because their desire has been bred into
most Americans through schools and social institutions. But, unlike
the traditional heroes, their desire for success leads to troublesome
dilemmas, and their "triumphs" are of such an ambiguous nature that
we question, rather than applaud, their achievements. Billy Pilgrim
starts with an unshakable belief in the sanctity of the American
family, an institution long dear to social and religious leaders. But
Billy finds only unhappiness with his families; the strength that
should theoretically support him is inadequate or nonexistent. Even
his rescue by Tralfamadore, because fantastic, underscores his failures with his earth families. The characters in *The Sting* begin with
the traditional belief that there should be equal justice for all, even
those who are seemingly beyond the law. But that attitude causes
serious problems, and the two con men end up rejecting the validity
of the traditional notion to assert that self-gratification is equally
important. Lauren and Daniel first embrace certain established concepts of romance. Lauren is captured by the ideas of Elizabeth
Barrett Browning, and places her hopes for happiness in an old
"legend" associated with the poetess; Daniel faithfully imitates the
attitudes of his favorite film heroes, aping them to the point that his
personality is submerged. Dedicated to their own particular ideals,
the adolescents pursue separate goals until it is almost too late to save
their relationship.

Once we recognize that Hill's films are not crass imitations of
traditional works, we can perceive the outline of the world present in
his films. In his universe the individual has become burdened with
cultural misconceptions. The culture has shaped his attitudes in such
a way that he or she can conceive of discovering meaning and attaining happiness only through the attainment of certain preordained
goals. For the character, prescribed rituals, such as the performance
of a heroic action, lead to the prescribed results of respect and
reward. The cultural concepts are so dominating that the individual
cannot conceive of alternatives, and thus the concepts occasionally
become more valuable than life itself. Further, Hill argues, the
concepts are antiquated, describing fixed relationships that no longer
apply to a fluid, changing world, and, at their worst, they absorb the
individual.

A review of the conflict in each film shows that it is the individual's
belief in a concept that is the source of trouble. Butch and Sundance
are trapped by their belief in the nobility of heroic individualism. The

nineteenth-century gentleman's code, as interpreted through American eyes, envisioned men whose moral probity was unquestioned, whose courage was unchallenged, whose stoicism, endurance, and strength were understood. Generous and heroic, the individual proved his right to adulation by his extraordinary feats, his capacity to perform beyond the abilities of ordinary men. He stood distinct from society and yet was an important element of it, and his success was his guarantee of personal bliss. Perhaps, as Mark Twain suggested, this concept came from the fevered writings of Sir Walter Scott, perhaps out of the manners and morals of the Victorian era, but, whatever its origins, the idea's influence cannot be doubted. The hero of innumerable Hollywood genre films embodied the same romantic characteristics, and society, through its emphasis on success, has always condoned and encouraged such qualities. Gifted achievers in sports, politics, and business were lauded as long as they maintained the external facade of a chivalrous gentleman.

Butch and Sundance, no matter how far they have drifted from the original model, still believe in and are motivated by the doctrine of individualism. They become criminals because it gives them the freedom to be distinct individuals and the opportunity to gain material wealth. The money allows them to play at and indulge in the role of the gentleman, and they find a camaraderie and a celebrated status that the more conventional figures, such as the marshall, do not. Not only do they enact the role of the individual hero, but they perpetually think in terms of it. Butch talks of joining up and fighting in the Spanish-American War. "We could be heroes," he says, envisioning in Boy Scout fashion a career where courage and gallantry would result in homage and reward. Such actions and remarks, while typically romantic, reveal an overwhelming naiveté, a misunderstanding of society in general and the war in particular. Dominated by their all-consuming belief in the doctrine of individuality, the outlaws can conceive of no other course of action than their present one; they persist in the same routines even as the world collapses around them, failing to see that the concept of individuality is a myth. Society may encourage personal endeavor, but it suppresses any unfettered individuality. The outlaws' reliance on crime to fulfill the myth is evidence that society provides no opportunities for the romantic spirit it fosters. Nor can they see that the structured technological society has resources beyond their strengths. Their fate is obvious, but they, unable to conceive of any alternatives to their lives, maintain the old ceremonies until the end.

Reggie Dunlop and Waldo Pepper are also enthralled by the idea of success. They believe, and their appeal as characters suggests that the audience believes, that success brings concomitant material and spiritual happiness. The homage enjoyed by the successful beckons them, and each in his own way wishes to attain some goal that will seemingly relieve his feelings of inadequacy or dissatisfaction. Such a desire seems second nature in a culture which almost indiscriminately lauds those who have achieved. Stories of spartan denial and dedication are part of the American mythology, and social institutions—religious, civic, and educational—have long urged men to strive for these ideals. For Waldo, happiness can only come when he can claim the title of "the best pilot in the world." For Reggie Dunlop, success means the championship and some apochryphally beautiful existence with a loving wife and adoring fans. This dreamworld, similar to the one fantasized by the moronic sportswriter and the broadcaster, captures Reggie, despite his intelligence. For both men, the goal is worth any sacrifice. Waldo gives up a relationship with Maudie and the possibility of real social contact with people to pursue this elusive dream. Reggie gives up his wife, abuses the emotions of the players, and insensitively uses Lily Braden for his own ends—all for an unrealizable success. The two are so obsessed that they cannot see the emptiness of their own lives and the pain that they cause others.

Billy Pilgrim is the most typically American of Hill's heroes, for he ardently believes in the supremacy of the family, the fundamentally strong and beautiful unit whose enshrinement in innumerable films reflects the cultural belief in its importance. The films of John Ford, for example, always posit the family as the locus of moral force and cultural strength. Billy accepts this belief, and *Slaughterhouse-Five* details his search for a family, first with Edgar Derby, then with Val, and finally with Montana. But the film also shows that the "families" are models of impotency (with Derby) and spiritual bankruptcy. Billy's willingness to disregard evidence to that effect is a measure of his blind devotion to the ideal, and an explanation of his persistent unhappiness. Since he cannot conceive of any alternative to the family, he suffers painfully with Val, Barbara, and Robert. Billy cannot escape his pain, and the triumph on Tralfamadore shows not so much the traditional strength of the family, but rather that the perfect family exists only in a fantasy, unattainable in our modern world.

At first glance, the con men heroes of *The Sting* seem atypical, but nonetheless their situation is generally analogous to that of other Hill protagonists. The difference is that only one character, Johnny Hooker, has anything approaching a conventional belief: a conviction that there can be equal justice for all. Success, such as his and Luther's, should be a proof of one's skill, intelligence, and manipulative ability—a mark of distinction in a particular trade. It should not be reached, as it is by Lonnegan, through cheating and murder. In order to revenge Luther, and, in effect, assert that all are subject to the same laws and rules, Hooker sets out to humiliate Lonnegan. He becomes an avenging angel, a guarantor of the equality and justice we all hold dear, who defeats the forces of Lonnegan and Lieutenant Snyder. But curiously his success is not brought about by a reliance on traditional beliefs and emotions; rather it comes through the manipulative skill and miraculous foresight of Gondorff, who is indifferent to revenge and justice.

In *A Little Romance,* the adolescents turn to cultural myths about love as an alternative to their own unhappy lives. Lauren is the child of an unstable family (her mother has married three times and appears headed for a fourth) and it is not surprising that her dream is of a permanent, eternal love. Part of the measure of her need is her ready acquiescence to the old con man's story, and her later willingness to risk all her happiness on fulfilling the requirements of his romantic tale. Equally important is Lauren's assumption that the answer to her problem already exists in the world, and that all she must do to achieve happiness is pass a certain test. Like the protagonists in Hill's other films, she focuses on a ritual rather than attempt to solve her problem through her own resources.

Daniel is much the same. His father is a nebulous presence, an oaf whom Daniel easily manages, and consequently he focuses on images of strong men capable of controlling their own destinies (the film characters of Bogart, Redford, Newman, Wayne, and Reynolds). In his search for a model adult male, he turns to those exemplars provided by our culture. There is nothing unusual in such an action, but Daniel's tenacious adherence to the attitudes expressed in those films, and his unwillingness to test or change these ideas, suggests some measure of Daniel's need for guidance. Like Lauren, he fixes on an idea, and interprets his experience in terms of it, clinging to it until it nearly costs him Lauren.

Characters so dominated by a concept lose their individuality; they play the role society expects and repress natural feelings in order to maintain a particular image. The outlaws become courteous, chivalrous, and gallant despite the incongruity of their profession with such

virtues, and maintain this facade even in times of danger. When
Butch Cassidy and Sundance retrieve the money from the Bolivian
bandits, they do so because the gentleman's code demands that they
honor their commitment to Percy Gariss, not because they enjoy
shooting people or are after the money. Common sense dictates that
they avoid such danger, but they act as they *feel* they should act, not
as the situation would seem to demand. Waldo Papper is also more
posture than person. His fabricated Kessler story is repeated not out
of vanity, but out of Waldo's desperate need to fulfill the outward
requirements of the individual hero role. He needs proof of his
greatness, and manufactures it when circumstances deny him the
opportunity to demonstrate his qualifications. The final battle is a
costumed sequence, and this fact only underscores the point that
Waldo plays a role that he finds satisfying. Reggie Dunlop also plays
various roles for different people, manipulating them for his own
ends. He plays the confident hero for his wife, projecting dreams of
imminent success that contrast with the depressing bleakness of his
situation. He plays a macho jock for Lily Braden, apparently because
he thinks it is appropriate for a sports hero, and consequently he
never moves past crudities with her. She exists only as a conquest, not
as a person. But his control of these personages is not complete, and
we see Reggie succumb to his own fantasies. This is clearest in the
sequence concerning the championship game. Reggie, who
throughout has seemed conscious of the folly of violent play, makes a
speech urging his players to play "old-time hockey." When, however,
he learns there are NHL scouts in attendance, he loses his perspective on violence and becomes another goon desperate for success in
sports, caught up in the dream he created to manipulate others. Billy
Pilgrim so desperately believes in the efficacy of the American family
that he goes through the motions of the traditional father role even
though his family is a hopeless shambles. Taking a cue from Edgar
Derby, Billy, as a good father, eternally praises and supports all that
goes on in his family. For example, he tells his Green Beret son that
he is proud of him, even though Robert's metamorphosis causes Billy
much more pain than pleasure. He defines himself through the father
role and exists as a complex of predetermined responses, not as a
person. With the teenagers of *A Little Romance*, Daniel plays roles
he has learned from films, acting a possessive, competitive male even
though his situation does not demand such efforts. Lauren dissem-
bles with Daniel, pretending she does not read Heidegger, or is not

afraid of pornographic films, or only wants an adventure with the trip to Venice; she also lies to Julius, pretending she wants to visit her sick mother. In each case her fear of opening up to others costs her; at first it is only momentary embarrassment, but at the porno house and on the trip to Venice the stakes are increased. The characters in *The Sting* adopt an endless series of personas to achieve their con of Lonnegan. They seldom drop the mask, not even for each other, for they have consciously realized what the other Hill characters intuitively know: that it is necessary to meet external requirements in order to meet goals. But the result is still the same in that the personality becomes submerged beneath the roles.

Once the difference in character and motivation are seen, the dynamics of Hill's counter story become clearer. As noted earlier, the characters begin as adherents of conventional American beliefs and move, because of their fidelity to those beliefs, to ambiguous resolutions of their problems. Such a filmic structure suggests the inadequacy of conventional views, for they cannot account for the changed, occasionally insensitive, sometimes threatening world the characters encounter. The conventional morality, accepted unthinkingly, is shown to be spiritually bankrupt; the roles it prescribes for individuals are now irrelevant, and it has no reserve resources to sustain its adherents.

Hill's films, then, juxtapose two understandings of the world. On the one hand there are the familiar genre narratives with their conventional metaphysics. The extraordinary success of his films indicates that the genre conventions have maintained their potency. The audience still finds American vitality, ingenuity, and skill attractive, and sees the qualities as tools that enable one to deal with the world. The characters seem familiar heroes, models whom we can safely emulate. But the films also show a world where conventional morality is false and inaccurate, hindering rather than helping the individual deal with the world. Characters who accept the fraudulent conventions dissipate their strengths in pursuit of illusory goals. Integrity, loyalty, skill, and courage are wasted in service to outworn ideals, and the individual, trapped by a system of unrealistic beliefs, is doomed to slow disintegration.

The two narratives, seen together, yield more than the naive optimism of the genre story or the cynicism of the genre variations. The second narrative reveals an ugly side of the first, forcing us to question conventional assumptions often taken for granted. We are asked to see that the frame of reference, the genre conventions, is no longer valid, and that a more complex understanding of the world must be arrived at.

Thus the films usually end on a negative note (*A Little Romance* is an exception), showing the disparity between the ideal (conventional assumptions) and the depressing reality in which individualism is impossible and characters are doomed by antiquated cultural beliefs. The films can be seen solely as a negative criticism of the culture for they do not suggest an alternative to the traditional understanding of the world. The majority of characters fail to come to terms with their problems or discover any potential solutions. But it is also possible to see the films as implicitly asserting the need for a new independence. The shock of recognition, the realization that Hill's criticisms are correct, may motivate some viewers to action. Instead of blindly accepting the dictates of others, the individual, in order to avoid the fate of Hill's characters, must learn to see with his own eyes, rely on his own judgments, and be willing to change.

2

Butch Cassidy and the Sundance Kid

BUTCH CASSIDY AND THE SUNDANCE KID (1969) is Hill's first cinematic triumph, for it demonstrates that he can intelligently explore and treat themes visually. The film takes a stock situation of the Western genre, the conflict between individuals and an advancing society, and by giving it a new shape fashions a comment on American society. The outlaws' story is as much the failure of romantic individualism as it is the triumph of technological society, for the outlaws' unwavering belief in the supremacy of the individual unwittingly brings them to their end. Instead of the traditional genre view that the individual is the dynamic force that prepares the road for and fosters the growth of society, only to be rejected because his individuality does not fit within the restrictions of civilization, *Butch Cassidy* shows that individuality has become a limiting, enervating cultural concept that ultimately absorbs rather than liberates the self. The outlaw heroes, we discover, are impotent to change. The mythic West is real to them, and they cling to their romantic, myopic view despite all contrary evidence. They continually act out the role of the heroic individual in order to resolve the increasingly complex problems of technological society rather than alter old ideas or test new ones. The conception has become perception; the need to be unrestricted, larger-than-life heroes dominates their minds, and all actions are interpreted according to this concept of self. Trapped by the roles, the outlaws become static and, in a world where flux is the norm, die. In Hill's Western, individualism is not so much out of place as it is outmoded.

Most critics would deny the film this depth. Reviewers found it "an enervated and sophisticated business venture,"[1] and claimed that

A legendary trio in an untypically formal pose (Katharine Ross,
Paul Newman, Robert Redford).
(Credit: Movie Star News)

"Hill and Goldman knew exactly what they were doing—making a very slick movie."[2] Especially criticized was the alleged lack of moral and artistic clarity. The reviewer from *Time* found it a mishmash of farce and tragedy, while Stanley Kauffmann and Pauline Kael suggested there was no hint of artistic focus.[3] Some claimed that the film was empty because we could not sympathize with the hollow, criminal characters. Kael found schoolteachers like Etta Place, who did honest work, more attractive than the outlaws, while Henry Hart claimed there was a "lot of anti-establishmentarian glamorizing of criminals," and "that beneath the kidding is the ideology, and some of the propaganda of today's nihilists."[4] Other reviewers criticized it on the ground that it had no feeling, no maturity, and no originality.[5] Those who did like it found it clever enough, and amusing, but not substantial. Hollis Alpert is typical with his comment that "George Roy Hill, following the plain lead of William Goldman's fine screenplay, is all fun and games."[6] No one thought the film a serious work.

All these criticisms seem to make one basic error; they judge the film by some fixed, external standard, not by the standards and boundaries the film creates for itself. Consider the claim that the film is suspect because it lacks a moral center and that, as Hart suggests, conscientious characters like Woodcock are more attractive than the amoral heroes.[7] This might be true in some external system, but it is certainly not true within the movie. Woodcock, we are made to see, fanatically and foolishly clings to his duties because he covets his job, not because of any abstract values. His tenacity evidences his shallowness, and he deserves to be laughed at. Pauline Kael argues that schoolteachers like Etta were more essential to the settling of the West, and are therefore more attractive than the outlaws and flaw the picture.[8] Perhaps schoolteachers were important to the settling of the West, but the film is not about the advance of civilization. When Etta goes with the outlaws, she goes because they offer a vitality that the town cannot. "All the excitement I've ever known is right here with me," she says at the moment of choice. Etta chooses, perhaps foolishly, an unordered world rather than the straitjacket of town life.

The most important rebuttal to the claim of immorality, however, is the outlaws' morality. Like Western heroes before them, they have a recognizable, attractive code of values. There is a concept of honor (Sundance's willingness to fight for his honor in the opening scenes) and responsibility (their actions with Percy Gariss). They accord respect to others who can survive in their world and ask only the same respect in return. And their reprehensible larceny appears attractive only if we ignore its debilitating nature. It would be more productive to focus on the subject that seems to attract both the audience and the director: the tension between the individuals and society. The outlaws' story offered Hill the opportunity to explore this perennially intriguing subject, and criticism should focus on his handling of that, not the details. *Butch Cassidy* is no more about bankrobbing than *Bonnie and Clyde*.

Most viewers enjoyed the film, unaffected by the critics' concerns, for it is a well-done, entertaining genre story. The outlaws and the posse are representative of two ways of life. The outlaws are clearly the traditional heroic individuals, persons who have declared their separateness from the sometimes entangling and leveling restrictions of society. The posse, physically and symbolically, is the force of the new, impersonal technological society. The physical struggle between the two groups becomes a metaphor for the struggle between the two ways of life. The posse's triumph signals the beginning of a new, less attractive world, a celebration of order at the expense of individuality; the film becomes an elegy to a way of life that has passed.

The genre story is clearly discernible, for Hill highlights the characters' representational status and the differences between the two groups. Butch and Sundance are presented as larger-than-life heroes, the incarnation of the West and its values. They exist throughout the film as almost legendary characters. The title sequence tells us that "they once ruled the West"; E. H. Harriman, the railroad magnate, hires a special posse to hunt them down as the last visible threat to the expanding society; the old sheriff identifies them as the last remnants of a dying race; Sundance's skill with a gun has earned him a larger-than-life identity; and the continual use of close-ups emphasizes their stature in relation to the other, almost anonymous characters in the film. Hill endows these characters with qualities that typify the old West. The outlaws survive and triumph through the use of individual skills. They are forthright, honorable, and courageous, loyally supporting and refusing to take advantage of each other. And, though never explicitly stated, these concepts form a code of values by which they live.

Arrayed against them are the men of the posse, the equally archetypal representatives of the new, impersonal society. Anonymous, mercenary, never clearly seen, attributed nearly superhuman powers by the other characters, they are clearly symbolic of the new order.[9] The leaders of this world, like the unseen E. H. Harriman, and the source of their power, the indistinct crowd in the town, are equally faceless and impersonal. The new citizens, like Woodcock, the payroll guard, live and fight for position in an organization rather than for themselves, and, as the failure of the marshall indicates, are indifferent to words like courage, honor, and responsibility.

Most viewers understandably sympathize with the outlaws, for they embody the qualities we desire and admire. We follow them, and suffer with them, and can find their death sad because we see in their refusal to yield to the new order a gallant, though futile gesture. *Butch Cassidy* (like *The Wild Bunch* and *The Shootist*) celebrates an elemental vitality that has been lost in the translation to technological society.

But in addition, Hill frustrates our stock expectations, creating an ambiguity that prevents identification and encourages a distanced, critical perspective on the outlaws and their actions. Once we move past the stock responses, we see that the story is ironic: the film, in exposing the weaknesses of the genre and its metaphysics, moves us from sympathy with the outlaws to a less emotional understanding of their failure. This is not to say the film parodies the genre, only that it examines it more carefully than is customary. It shows the limitations of unchallenged cultural conventions and implicitly urges a new independence: freedom from the chains of ideas, whether they be as restrictive as those of the advancing technological society, or as lulling, but ultimately false, as those of an older world.

The ironic perspective results from Hill's disruption of our stock responses, and this occurs from the beginning. The title sequence, a throwaway in many commercial films, here establishes the ambiguity prevalent in the outlaws' world, and forces us to think before committing our sympathies. Purportedly an old newsreel of the Cassidy gang in action, the sequence shows the outlaws robbing a train and then being foiled by a posse. It not only presages the chase sequence in the center of the film, but is also a cinematic allusion to Edwin S. Porter's *The Great Train Robbery*, the prototypical Western film. The situation is the same in the newsreel and in Porter's film, and even some of the shots are similar (the passengers are lined up and robbed in each; a passenger is shot in the Porter film, a guard in the newsreel) in camera placement and composition. However, in the Porter film and the genre that springs from it, people act out of understandable motives; moral values are clear, and rewards and punishments distributed according to that fixed value system. Thus, we know the gang in *The Great Train Robbery* deserves punishment because they have, by shooting an unarmed passenger, proved their cowardice and immorality. We cheer when they have been captured or killed and the world set right again. In Hill's sequence, the outlaws appear to be bandit heroes. They shoot the guard only because he tried to obtain unfair advantage, another cowardly action that violates the standard moral code. The audience prepares to respond to them until they are cast as villains by the appearance of the posse, who break up the robbery. But the resolution is ambiguous. The posse fails to capture the outlaws; the outlaws fail to complete the robbery; and we are left with an inconclusive puzzle that refuses to be solved by any standard emotional response. The title sequence is a tonal rubric of the film. The ambiguities produced by the variations in genre format serve as the first indication that we are not in cinematically familiar territory.

The opening scenes of the film proper grow out of the title sequence in that they continue to develop the sense of ambiguity found there. These sepia-toned scenes appear to be common commercial fare, introducing us to heroes who are likeable and extraordinarily skilled. Yet, if we look carefully, we find that Hill has controlled the cinematic elements to suffuse the scenes with a nonstandard sensibility. In the first shot, the camera follows Butch as he cases a bank and then jokes about the bank's formidable security; the joke works (for most viewers) and the humor that is Butch's hallmark is established. However, the visual elements undercut the ease and humor of the scene. The film opens with a rack through focus from a window to a shot of Butch behind a barred window. The association with jail is unavoidable, even though Butch overturns it by stepping out into the street a moment later. Inside the bank, the prison association continues. As Butch stands in the center of the bank, glancing at the various security paraphernalia, Hill cuts from the bolts, doors, and windows, slamming and shutting, to Butch's face, which is gradually becoming darker. The montage effect suggests Butch as the one being enclosed and imprisoned. The sense of foreboding is broken by Butch's joke, but the visual content of the scene remains negative; it creates an ambiguous tension, parallel to that of the title sequence, that retards the affective impulse usually accompanying such scenes.

We are then introduced to the Sundance Kid, a more recognizable Western hero. In the duel of nerves with the card dealer, Sundance demonstrates the self-assurance and extraordinary skill expected, winning an immediate and favorable audience response. The visual and dramatic content, however, conveys additional information that

alters our understanding of the traditional scene. The juncture between this and the opening scene is the first hint that there is another
dimension. As the guard closes the door on Butch, the camera rests
just long enough for us to hear the latch closing. There is then a direct
cut to Sundance's face, a shift that joins the connotations of the first
scene to the second. Further, if we note the composition, we find a
visual comment on the nature of the outlaws' world. Sundance is
framed by the shoulders of the card players, thus rendering him
explicit and them anonymous. We see the dealer's face only for a
moment, when he learns of Sundance's identity. Such composition
suggests something of the anonymous nature of the outlaws' oppo-
nents, and in a small way prepares the groundwork for the posse.
Finally, we have Butch's facetious comment that Sundance may be
"over the hill." The line becomes funny in light of Sundance's performance, but it also introduces the idea of being overtaken, of failing
to survive, that is central to the film.

The first two scenes, then, do more than introduce our heroes.
First, the base of one of the film's main themes, the passing of an era,
is set in the bank and in Butch's comment. Second, since they are shot
in a sepia tone, the scenes induce a nostalgic sense of identification
with the past; however, there is a concomitant, though less distinct
suggestion that the men and the qualities they represent are extinct.
Third, the contrast between the visual element and the dramatic
element creates an ambiguity that prevents total identification with
the heroes. And fourth, the limitations of the outlaws are outlined for
us. As the movie progresses, we discover that the outlaws never go
beyond the qualities demonstrated here. They always resolve problems by wit or by skill with a gun; for them, it is an individual
encounter in an arena, and they never seem able to grasp larger
concepts or issues. The opening shots fully develop them.

The movie now shifts to color, but it still develops, by a process of
accretion, the ideas suggested in the sepia scenes. We are shown
something attractive or humorous, that draws our sympathies for the
outlaws, but which also contains shadings that suggest potential
dangers or the limitations of the characters. The commercial entertainment takes on an added substance that transforms the stereotypes
into characters and the stock plot into a vehicle for exploring ideas.
Consider, for example, the sequence which follows them back to their
camp. The shots show the magnificent countryside, the harsh, yet
promising landscape that is part of the American myth of the West.
The dialogue affirms that the struggle is between these two classic
Western heroes and the changing society, and it reveals the affable

humanity of the characters. The talk of Bolivia demonstrates that the outlaws are searching for another place to live, thus making their move there plausible later, and shows that they have some understanding of their situation.

But on another level the dialogue shows that the outlaws' understanding of their situation is superficial and incomplete, and also that this lack is as important as the confrontation with society. Butch simplistically equates Bolivia with the California of 1849, and this equation indicates that, for Butch, an El Dorado always exists, a dreamland where he can enjoy his present life-style. The problem for him is *not* one of accepting the changes encountered; it is one of finding another pastoral locale in which he can avoid the problems of change. Butch and Sundance fear change because they cannot comprehend the consequences of it and remain adamant in their refusal to change. Their present existence seems benevolently ordered for their own greatest good. Their paradise provides everything, and they have ample opportunity to demonstrate their rugged individuality. Simply by taking from others they satisfy their need for pleasure, money, status, and self-sufficiency. And, incredibly, such an effort has been blessed by the peculiar circumstances of the time; their ability to survive and prosper on the frontier has made them heroes. No wonder the past holds such attraction for them.

They seem determined to exist there, as their dialogue indicates. When Sundance laughs at the outlandishness of Bolivia, Butch deprecatingly pokes fun at himself. "Boy," he says, "I've got vision; the rest of the world's got bifocals."[10] This ironic comment was meant to show Butch's understanding, but there is another edge to it as well. Butch may josh about his ideas, but when it comes to the acid test he embraces them: he goes to Bolivia and chases his dream. He may sense that his understanding is incomplete, may joke about it, but he will not make an effort to correct it. The attractions of the past exert too great a hold on him. Sundance's laugh and dismissal of the remark with a shrug indicate a similar weakness on his part. He acts only when physically threatened; otherwise he is content to let events, thoughts, and insights pass him by. Unless confronted with something concrete, Sundance, pure response, cannot deal with the world around him. He is limited by his perception of what is important (his honor and his survival), content to let others lead him, and unwilling to question himself or his world.

The exchange introduces a new dimension to their struggle, for we see that the outlaws are ill-equipped to deal with the advancing society. Their childishly naive understanding of the world is so superficial as to be unacceptable; it seems founded on some vague conceptions of an Edenic past. In traditional films, as Michael Wood points out, there is never any question of the *value* of individuality, only its *place* in relation to society.[11] Here, the individuality associated with the outlaws is problematical; it seems incapable of dealing with the world. Central to this questioning is the problem of vision, to use the language of Butch's metaphor. We realize that their survival depends on the clarity with which they see, and, if this scene is an indication, their perspicuity is sadly lacking. As the film progresses, we find them continually limited by their inability to see beyond the outlines of a romantic myth, and the question of their perceptual acuity becomes as much a part of the film as does the elegy to their lost way of life.

The scenes with Harvey and the first train robbery well illustrate the importance of perception. Most viewers see them as entertaining incidents, laughing as Butch outwits Harvey and Woodcock, and strengthening their identification with the bandits. But the scenes also reveal the increasing pressure on the outlaws' world: internally, from the members of the gang, and externally, from the new organization man. Woodcock delays the robbery for only a few seconds, but his motive, love of place in an organization, is a veiled warning to the outlaws. And, of course, the scenes show the outlaws are unable to comprehend the danger to their idyllic world.

This inability is evidenced in the scene with Harvey, in which Butch defeats the clod with some fast talk and a kick to the groin. It is generally humorous, but one shot suggests another response. Hill disturbs our perception of the scene, disrupting our stock response, by having a "screen" of dust flow between the characters and the camera; he asks, in effect, that we exert ourselves in order to see the scene. We are given a medium close-up of Butch's face as he spins a line about needing to spend more time in town. As he speaks, a cloud of dust passes in front of him, obscuring Harvey from him and him from us—a visual metaphor for Butch's clouded vision. He cannot see that Harvey represents something beyond mere physical danger, nor that circumstances are forcing him to spend more time in town. To him it is only a challenge, another opportunity to prove his individual ability to survive. He cannot or will not see events as anything other than a continuing chapter in an endless fairy tale.[12]

The scene with Woodcock serves as a similar reminder. Woodcock's inept bungling induces laughter as the genre hero encounters the buffoon. But once we reflect on the scene, the stock response again proves inadequate. Woodcock foreshadows something dangerous. His willingness to die for an organization is representative of the lack of individuality and the desire for anonymity that will doom the outlaws. Butch, with his comment that "all that matters is that we come out ahead," reduces the situation to an I-win-you-lose formula; he deals with the present, and cannot move beyond the immediate. To most in the audience he remains attractive, but as he stands in the swirling smoke (perhaps accidental, but perhaps seized upon by Hill for use as a metaphor), he remains undeniably limited.

The town sequence that follows emphasizes the same point. On the one hand the scene is funny, with the cuts between the fatuous marshall and the relaxing outlaws; on the other hand it indicates the serious dangers that must be faced and the outlaws' lack of comprehension of them. The subtle shift in attitude indicated by the marshall's failure is frightening. He cannot raise a posse with appeals to duty, individual responsibility, or self-respect because the people in the town find these ideas meaningless. The apathetic crowd is representative of the new sheep, people who retreat into anonymity and the safety of the group. They have relinquished their individuality for the guarantee of safety and contrast sharply with the outlaws, who are still willing to fight for their honor. The threat such an attitude represents, the massed power of such blank mindless force, though minimized by laughter, should not be ignored.

The second threat is the bicycle salesman, with his machine "that won't do much—only change the course of your lives." Butch indulges childishly in the novelty of the bike and does not see that the new technology is altering the West. The third element is less obvious. The dialogue between the two men reveals a naiveté, an unthinking belief in nineteenth-century romanticism, that will always have difficulty dealing with the world. Butch suggests joining up and fighting in the Spanish-American War; "We could be heroes," he says. The comment evidences such a simplistic picture of war and the world that even Sundance reacts; he bursts the bubble by saying Butch is too old. Butch is angered, so Sundance backs off and restores peace. Butch cannot accept criticism because it implies error and is an implicit challenge to the perfection of his daydream world. Sundance cannot be bothered with anything other than his immediate situation; he seems to hope indifference will dissipate his problems. Their tolerance for each other keeps the relationship smooth, but it should not prevent us from seeing the extent of their limitations.

Next comes the bike-riding scene, carefree and joyous, with its bright colors, soft-focus photography, and lyric music. Yet even in the midst of it, detail indicates that the outlaws will not be able to maintain this bliss. As Butch and Etta roll under the trees, Etta picks off an apple, takes a bite, and hands it to Butch. Associations with the Garden of Eden and a fall from paradise come to mind, particularly when we consider that the happiness stressed through color, music, and photography is taking place aboard a bike, the symbol of a new era. The means of destruction has already entered the paradise. In addition, another "screen," this time of blossoms, obtrudes and slightly obscures our vision during the last exchange of dialogue. The "screen" suggests again that the action needs more than a superficial glance to be understood. Butch tells Etta that a shortage of money necessitates another robbery, a problem Etta suggests is caused by Butch's foolish, spendthrift ways. He shrugs in agreement and moves on through the blossoms, ever unwilling to consider the implications. He cannot "see" the problem because his internal perception is as blurred as the physical.

At this point, the film has developed the outlaws' character, both strengths and weaknesses, and outlined the nature of the forces arranged against them. The film has demonstrated their admirable qualities, inducing almost total identification with them, and thus allowing us to share in their happiness and gaiety. Also, we align ourselves with them in the seemingly clear-cut struggle against the encroaching society. Yet the attractiveness and simplicity covers a more complex situation. The movie dissociates us from the outlaws by constantly reminding us that there is something intrinsically awry with their way of living. The outlaws' continuing inability to comprehend the world around them interferes with our simple emotional response. In addition, not only has each scene contributed to our awareness of their limitations, but the sequence of situations, the narrative structure, suggests that their world is slowly disintegrating. They move from less to more threatening situations, a structural progression that parallels and underscores the gradual erosion of their world. By the time of the bicycle sequence, there is a tension that must be resolved, and it is apparently done in the chase sequence. That reaffirms the outlaws' humanity, and gives an old answer to the problem of encroaching society: flight to less developed lands. The trip to New York City and the Bolivian robbery sequence seem the realization of that traditional possibility. But, as always, Hill undercuts their triumph, showing instead that they are only proceeding in the same self-destructive direction. The shootout with the army in Bolivia is simply a substitute for the shootout with the posse, a moment they have been able to delay, not escape.

Their struggle at first calls forth the audience's sympathy. As the posse becomes more resolute, the outlaws become more human and accessible, suffering reversals, and becoming tired, dirty, and drawn. Their extraordinary skills fail them, and they escape only by virtue of chance, a quality that heroes rise above. In contrast to their humanity stands the abstract nature of the posse; it seems pure presence, the antithetical force that opposes all outlaws. We first see the engine of its train, shot in low or odd angles to emphasize its size and power, and presented in a montage of parts to point out its impersonality. The posse disgorged from the train takes on these same qualities. Its skill and power are evidenced through the quick killing of the two outlaws, and their impersonality through the series of extreme long shots. The camera draws farther and farther away until they become a series of lights, a cloud of dust on the horizon. In some sequences there is only a shot of the landscape, recently traversed by the outlaws, and a sound, something like distant thunder, which suggests the presence of the pursuing force. The outlaws' questions—"Who are those guys?" "Don't they ever quit?" "Why don't they do something different?"—only emphasize the metaphoric nature of the posse. It has become the physical incarnation of the technological society, the threat of death.

But the chase sequence also reveals the fundamental limitations of the characters. The sequence begins with a comic set piece, the second encounter with Woodcock, that subtly points out the growing danger and the outlaws' obliviousness to it. There is laughable confusion in the explosion and the chase for money, but in the more formidable safe lies another threatening technological development. The ubiquitous dust cloud is again present as the outlaws remain insensitive to the veiled threat of the safe. After the chase gets underway, the insensitivity seems to increase rather than decrease. This is perhaps clearest in the scene with the old sheriff. They offer to trade their banditry for army commissions, an idea so absurd the sheriff scoffs. "Your times is dead," he tells them. "All you can do is choose where you're going to die." The outlaws, true to form, refuse to accept the increasingly obvious judgment and sheepishly depart. But we cannot ignore the accuracy of that insight, for the action in the rest of the sequence confirms the sheriff's assertion. Butch tries trick after trick, with equal ineffectiveness, but still refuses to believe that his skills will not somehow save him. He cannot grasp the totality of his situation because his mind has rejected the possibility of failure or surrender. In his life and his romantic conceptions, success always

"Lovable, charming outlaws" with a "seemingly limitless capacity for bad judgment"
during two tense adventures.
(Courtesy: Museum of Modern Art/Film Stills Archive).

follows a great individual effort, and so he retains a blind faith in the certainty of his own triumph. To him the posse is only a more difficult test than his encounters with Harvey and Woodcock. They ultimately escape, but only through a desperation leap that delays, but does not eliminate, a confrontation with the new force. However, they see the escape as some natural extension of their luck. Rather than change, they decide to go to Bolivia. For them, it is still a problem of locale, not one of vision or conception of the world. Etta knows this is self-deception, but our heroes push blindly backward in spite of her.

The second half of the film parallels the first. The outlaws draw our sympathies, but also reveal the same weaknesses that repelled us earlier. We see that they are doomed and remain victims of their romantic mythology. There are two long entertaining visual sequences that captivate the audience and simultaneously reveal that the weaknesses have not been shed in the transition from America to Bolivia.

In the city sequence we follow the outlaws from the slowly turning bike wheel, the symbol of the new era, which Butch has rejected, to New York, the center of the new world. The trio is immensely attractive as they toy with turn of the century New York, indulging themselves in its amusements, posturing and posing—children on a holiday. Their attractiveness arises from the fact that they view the 1890s as a fantasy world to be enjoyed, not something to be taken seriously. And the technique of the sequence underscores this fact. The stills, the montage, the lively music, the locations—amusement galleries and public parks—and the sepia tone all seem to flow together to create a sense of spontaneity and fun that is part of the outlaws' character. But even so, that should not prevent us from seeing that they are incapable of dealing with New York except as a dreamworld. They cannot survive here, and must move backward, as the right to left motion of the train indicates, to the pastoral locale of Bolivia.[13]

The bank robbery sequence in Bolivia is another superb example of Hill's ability to combine concrete narrative detail and abstract thematic statement into entertaining fare. We follow the outlaws as they progress from bumbling amateurs and regain their status as first-class robbers. In a few minutes of film time, they gain the same notoriety and success that were the subject of the first half of the film. Other shots, though, remind us that the outlaws, despite all their success, are still on the same treadmill. In one robbery sequence the camera focuses not on their cleverness, but on a bound bankguard, and follows his gaze as he looks from the outlaws to a poster for "Bandidos

Yanquis." Their pastoral locale becomes another arena for a confrontation between the outlaws and the forces of the society. Once again they have inadvertently created a potentially destructive situation. Another shot shows the outlaws escaping from the soldiers with a variation of the "Sweetface" ruse, the same trick that failed them in their chase with the posse. They have not moved forward; simply fallen back into their old patterns, complete with the same tired ruses that will ultimately fail again. When the sequence finishes, the intimation is confirmed. Etta and the outlaws are forced from a luxury dinner by the sighting of a white skimmer, a trademark of the man who led the posse. This is a final revelation of their doom. The audience knows that it is implausible, but the outlaws, haunted by a self-projected fear, are trapped into the same old response of flight. We realize now that they are fated to repeat the same scenario, always the victims of their own projections.

They decide to go straight, but their romantic conceptions make it a futile gesture. They still must fulfill the requirements of the code, only they discover it now to be an empty and unsatisfying experience. Instead of metamorphosis, they cloak the old self with a new costume, that of payroll guards for Percy Gariss. When he gets shot, they are put in the novel position of avenging a crime, for they feel they must honor their commitment to him. This leads them to a shootout with the bandits in which Butch reaches perhaps the nadir of his career when for the first time he is forced to shoot another man. The slow motion filming emphasizes the violence, reflecting Butch's horror at the killings. The finality of his descent is then underscored as a cloud of dust moves in front of his face and a sound, like distant thunder, is faintly heard. Butch still cannot see the significance of his experiences; he remains haunted by the posse, his avenues of escape slowly disappearing. Etta's departure soon after fulfills her prophecy that she would not watch them die.

The process of disintegration is quickly concluded. We see the outlaws reduced to jungle work, bickering with each other, and eating cheap meals in dirty towns. They have reached the end of their journey, and the shootout is a logical conclusion to the film. In that final battle, we see the essential paradox of their lives. Their strengths and attractive qualities, derived from the code of the hero, prevent them from clearly seeing their situation or doing anything about their occasionally gleaned insights. Even though they are doomed, they play the role, gallantly fulfilling the gentleman's code by maintaining a brave and indifferent facade in the midst of danger. They talk again, in the same half-mock, half-serious tone with which they talked of Bolivia, of new adventures. But the code, which has no applicability except perhaps in moments of danger, prevents them from ever going beyond that half-mocking tone. They go to their deaths, misinterpreting their immediate situation and oblivious to the larger context of their lives.

The film ends as an indictment of the American concepts of heroism and individuality. The disappearance of the individual, the film suggests, was caused as much by the nature of the idea as by the advancing society. The American West, so often associated with individualism, serves as the focal point of this study. Hill introduces figures who seem archetypal incarnations of the Western hero: courageous, gallant, talented, affable, and free from restraint, creators and masters of their own world. But he also shows the flaw in this ideal. In achieving their individuality, the characters have sacrificed the ability to respond and grow with the changing situations. The image has trapped the man. They feel they must play a hero's role and perform in certain ways, or else lose their feeling of worth. Even though the role no longer accords with reality, they cling to it, for they can conceive of no alternatives. In accepting the anachronistic concept of individuality, Butch and Sundance have cut themselves off from the flow of life. Their inability to comprehend anything except in terms of this individual mystique makes them easy victims of technological society.

The perceptive viewer can see that American individualism, in addition to its immense attractiveness, has an inherent weakness, a preoccupation with the concerns of role that prevents growth. Somehow, the film suggests, we must enlarge our field of vision so that pursuit of dreams does not become a selfish, self-limiting, self-defeating struggle.

Butch Cassidy is Hill's first film to go beyond genre limitations, using the familiar material as part of a new creation, an incisive examination of the culture's fundamental assumptions. It marks a new stage of growth and maturity in Hill's career, commercially and artistically, one that continues in his next film, *Slaughterhouse-Five*.

3

Slaughterhouse-Five

BILLY PILGRIM, the American dreamer in Hill's *Slaughterhouse-Five* (1972), searches for the security and happiness that participation in the dream supposedly provides. He fails to find it, however, in a world that contains the horror of Dresden and the stultifying vapidness of Ilium, and instead retreats to the paradise of Tralfamadore. He finds life there eminently satisfying, for it seems at last an affirmation of the American Dream. On Tralfamadore, respect, kindness, courtesy, and love help relieve suffering and create the spiritual happiness that serves as an alternative to the shallow, materialistic world of Ilium.

Slaughterhouse-Five, then, seems to be another statement of conventional wisdom in its insistence that a return to spiritual values brings happiness. The film follows Billy Pilgrim, the archetypal American, born on the Fourth of July, as he attempts to bring his search for happiness to a successful end. It follows him as he accepts the ideals of Edgar Derby, the incarnation of small-town American goodness, and then discovers the inadequacy of Derby's idealism in a harsh, modern world. The film follows Billy as he converts to the ideals of the American material dream, the equation of material success with happiness. But, as the film humorously and satirically points out, that life is a false and shallow existence, hardly worth the having. It follows him as he finally escapes to Tralfamadore, where the timeless spiritual values of family and basic decency serve as a base upon which to build happiness.

So constructed, the film seems a satire of modern American life and an affirmation of traditional American values. It rips apart one American dream, that of material success, and asserts the supremacy of

Billy Pilgrim poses in a mystical mood.
(Credit: Movie Star News)

another, the ascendancy of basic spiritual and family values. Most of
the critics who liked the film agreed that this affirmation of traditional
values was one of the film's enjoyable attributes.[1] But the film is more
properly a savage attack on the spiritual poverty of the American
culture. While presenting what seems a familiar story, Hill adds and
alters elements to jolt the viewer from a comfortable, conventional
perception of the story and character. Hill creates a discrepancy
between what we see and what we expected to see, encouraging the
perceptive viewer to probe the American myth of success.

In so doing, we discover that Billy Pilgrim is transformed from the
stereotype of a bumbling, good-natured, common man into a complex character troubled by his painful memories of the war. His war
experiences—his confrontation with suffering, his recognition
(through the death of Derby) of his own mortality, and the responsibility that he, as an American, must somehow share for the senseless
slaughter of the war—have become obdurate problems which resist
his efforts at resolution. Uncharacteristically, the American culture
which he so unwaveringly embraces fails to help him; its values
provide no satisfactory solution, and Billy turns instead to a world of
fantasy. Hill shows Billy as a dreamer whose longings for security and
happiness, seemingly unattainable in Dresden or Ilium, drive him to
create Tralfamadore, a world of the mind to which he can retreat. His
need to resort to fantasy becomes a measure of his and the culture's
limitations, and the configuration of the fantasy (Tralfamadore is
basically America) suggests something of the culture's destitution.
The values of family and virtue are not so much affirmed as attacked,
forcing us to reexamine those tenets which seem central to the
American ethic.

The exploration of America's culture is one of two ways in which
Hill's film differs from Kurt Vonnegut's novel. In the book, Billy
Pilgrim (and the other characters, Edgar Derby, Paul Lazzaro, and
Val Pilgrim) are passive victims of a universe which routinely subjects
people to grotesque, macabre, and cruel jokes. They seldom comprehend the horror or foolishness of their situation, and consequently
their reactions are the habits acquired from their separate environ-
ments. The firebombing of Dresden is not an extraordinary event for
them, and Vonnegut's matter-of-fact description, which is exactly like
his description of routine events, emphasizes the characters' dullness
and limitations. In the film, however, Hill elaborates on the characters, consciously making Billy and Edgar Derby active, vocal propo-
nents of traditional American values. Billy has clearly defined goals
toward which he works, and he has beliefs which he uses as a defense

against the horrors of Dresden. The question of the "proper" way to act is more important to the characters in the film than the nebbishes in Vonnegut's book, and consequently it is of more importance to the audience as well. Hill uses Billy's advocacy of these traditional values to develop a theme which is central to his work, but one which is not as important to Vonnegut.

A second difference between the book and the film is the sense of humor. Vonnegut's humor can be characterized as ironic, grotesque, or absurd, involving gruesome violence arbitrarily inflicted on unsuspecting victims. The flat descriptions of often horrorific incidents further emphasize the absurdity of the universe. Hill's film is more traditional in that the humor arises our of the conflict between a rigid attitude (Val's middle-class values or the army's rules) and someone (usually Billy) who threatens to invert that attitude. Since Hill relies more on incongruity than grotesque physical suffering, the humor is gentler and less ironic.

For the most part, however, Hill's film remains faithful to Vonnegut's novel. Hill and screenwriter Stephen Geller adopt the book's basic narrative and even a few crucial lines of dialogue. More importantly, Hill has captured the spirit of Vonnegut's novel, showing, like Vonnegut, that our society is incapable of coping with the horror of war except by ignoring or diminishing it. This probing of the illusions which society uses to sustain itself is basic to the work of both men, and it is perhaps this reason that *Slaughterhouse-Five*, while remaining true to its source, is a work of art in its own right.

Character Development

Initially, Hill establishes Billy Pilgrim as a sympathetic and readily identifiable American character: the naif. Billy is the classic rube who makes good, attaining a success others thought beyond him or willfully tried to deny him.[2] He has many limitations, a condition with which we can all identify, but none that interfere with his attainment of happiness. His career becomes a proof that the common man, despite the lack of extraordinary intelligence, physical prowess, or heroic character can eventually triumph.

The film develops Billy's character in traditional style, and the story rarely departs from his experiences. We begin witnessing events from his perspective, the camera inside the house, following his screeching daughter. The composition and staging always focus on Billy; we follow him when he leaves a group and focus on him within a group. Several scenes converge upon or expand from Billy, the camera moving in to or out from him for a close-up, suggesting that he is the center of the filmic universe. For example, Hill cuts from the collapsed Billy in the British prisoner of war barracks to the sleeping Billy on the lawn in Ilium, or from Billy on Tralfamadore whispering to Montana to Billy in the foxhole whispering similar words.

But this central position alone does not warrant our sympathy; Billy earns that because of his character. In his relationship with Montana, for example, Billy is strong, courteous, and gentlemanly. In his indifference to tangible wealth, he seems a spiritual pilgrim, someone searching for permanent values to oppose to the temporary material values of Ilium. His patience with and consideration for Val and Robert, his good nature, and his childlike innocence all reinforce his saintliness.

Comparison with other characters heightens these qualities. Lazzaro, Billy's principal tormentor, is a vicious, cowardly psychopath whose inhumanity stands in marked contrast to Billy's endless gentleness. The arrogance and posturing of Lazzaro, such as the nonsense about the Detroit Tigers, are constantly undercut by Billy's naivete. And Lazzaro's lack of honor, evidenced in the scene with Campbell, also helps push our sympathy toward Billy. Lazzaro, although a caricature, highlights Billy's character. The Pilgrim family provides another counterpart. Val is an exaggeration of the bourgeois housewife obsessed with status climbing and the outward trappings of success. Her constant squealing over Cadillacs and diamonds and her sexless attire increase our sympathies for Billy, while the puritanical self-righteousness of Val and Barbara and Robert's truculency make Billy seem intelligent, moderate, and human.

Finally, Billy evokes our sympathy because he suffers unfairly at the hands of an incomprehensible fate. He seems unjustly put upon by his war experiences and, to a lesser extent, his family. Though the horror of the firebombing of Dresden can only be minimally suggested on camera, we sense that its effect was devastating. The grotesquerie of mere survival, of the search for and the burning of bodies, and the senseless death of Derby all contribute to a nightmare that haunts Billy after the war's close. Billy also suffers in Ilium, although on a more limited scale. He is surrounded by people who have no conception of what he has endured. His mother and Mr. Rosewater talk of Dresden in an insincere garden-party tone; the doctor who administers the shock treatments talks as if giving a lecture: "Billy was in Dresden during the war . . . and it's only natural to assume it's had some effect on him." At home, life is equally painful. In the wedding-night sequence, Val crawls all over the inert

Billy, smothering him with kisses, cooing the romantic and moral conventions of the forties. "I'm so glad we waited . . . you've had experiences in the war, but I understand. . . ." For her, married life is a succession of salads and shortcakes; the children something to show off to her girl friends; the gifts of diamonds and cars, and Billy's success, so many badges of status; and Billy some kind of addendum that fills out a perfect life. She is incapable of seeing that Billy is unhappy in his own home, a stranger whose only friend is his dog; she cheerfully converts his painful wartime experiences into conversational topics, insensitively driving Billy away.

If Billy's character is recognizable and sympathetic, his actions are also familiar. Billy is a searcher (as the name Pilgrim implies) for those spiritual values which will make life worthwhile and happiness possible. At first he seeks to integrate himself into society; later, he seeks to integrate his war experiences into his civilian life, to free himself from the memories of suffering and death. Others in the war are not so troubled, Lazzaro and Weary are certain of who they are ("We're Americans," Weary confidently explains); the British major in the prisoner of war camp has his litany of bowel evacuation and teeth brushing to sustain himself; and Howard Campbell, the superpatriot from Vonnegut's earlier novel *Mother Night,* so fanatical that he has apparently become a Nazi, is spurred by his hatred of communism and by his conviction that the world would be right should we eliminate Russians and Jews. But Billy is different. He has experienced firsthand and cannot forget the brutality of the senseless human suffering at Dresden. He can never escape the consciousness that meaningless pain was inflicted on human beings by other human beings. In this way, he is analogous to his hospital companion, Rumford. When Rumford is confronted with a living reminder of the human pain and suffering at Dresden, he cannot rationalize it and lapses into shallow, bombastic political crudities. Billy, who continually confronts the specter of suffering in his own memories, cannot afford the luxury of mere speechmaking. He must find another means of understanding his experiences. He makes two wrongheaded lurches toward this goal before he eventually sets himself in the right direction. The audience suffers with Billy as he first follows the Boy Scout idealism of Edgar Derby and then the materialism of middle America, and then identifies with Billy when he embraces Tralfamadore.

Billy's search is established at the beginning of the film. The long shots of him stumbling through the snow stress his isolation and emphasize his insignificance. He seems lost in the infinite white expanse. His experiences in the foxhole reveal that his isolation and dislocation are spiritual as well as physical. Billy does not fit in with the cartoon strip world of Lazzaro, which is filled with forties' war movie clichés such as baseball players, dog tags, love of guns, and fanatical courage. Equally obvious is Billy's sense of the difference. "You guys go on without me," he constantly tells them, apparently used to the chasm between himself and his fellow soldiers. The difference is further manifested in Billy's malleability. People continually single him out, sensing that he has not yet solidified his character, and is therefore manipulable. Lazzaro feeds on Billy's weakness, knowing that he at least will be intimidated by his vicious rhetoric. The German soldiers single Billy out for the woman's coat, and the German photographer finds Billy the perfect conquered American. The British prisoner of war senses that Billy needs special knowledge to understand his role in the war and spares no effort to enlighten him. The whores in the window spot Billy's naiveté, and the children of Dresden find him a kind of magical creature for their games. And Wild Bob, who can get no one else to listen to him, manages to transform Billy into the best shot in the legendary 451st. For his part, Billy happily complies with the impositions, smiling sheepishly whenever he pleases anyone, regardless of uniform or intentions. He has no identity, and consequently revels in whatever role is offered him, doing almost anything for a little acceptance. As his attire, the woman's coat and the silver boots, indicates, not even the armies of Germany and America can mold him; as his actions indicate, this special status would gladly be traded for admission into society.

Billy's search for acceptance, though, is not haphazard. As the scenes with Derby demonstrate, he has a definite goal in mind. For Billy, happiness seems to consist of the mythical small-town values that Derby symbolizes. Derby, the honest, decent, hardworking, upstanding, productive member of the community, is fiercely patriotic, devoted to his family, and an exemplar of sexual restraint and fidelity. He sincerely believes and acts on the values and ideals upon which America was founded. For example, he constantly points out the German violations of the Geneva convention, confident that they only need a friendly reminder to correct them; and he endlessly supports anything American. When Lazzaro gets out of line, Derby tells him that "we Americans have got to stick together." When Billy reveals his disappointment in his henpecked father, Derby tells him to "never sell him short."

Billy obviously idolizes the man and his ideals. The time with Derby is the only part of Billy's life in which he demonstrates any enthusiasm, for in Derby he has found a father to guide him. Derby (whom Lazzaro calls "Pop") leads Billy's thoughts and actions, by example—during the election of the prisoner of war leader—or by rhetoric—as in the confrontation with Campbell. He also protects Billy from the marauding Lazzaro. There is a spiritual bond established in the scenes between the two men. Billy calls Derby the "greatest father in the world" because of the open affection Derby displays for his son. When Billy explains hé became an optometrist to help others, Derby applauds the sentiment: "That's self-determination and free enterprise backing itself up all the way! That's why we're here in Europe fighting Hitler!" When Derby is elected to lead the prisoners of war, Billy is his only supporter. The cross-cuts between Derby's election and Billy's election to the Lions Club, as well as the similarity of their speeches, emphasize the relationship between the two men.

And so Billy joins Derby in a celebration of the American virtues. But, the film suggests, such confidence has been misplaced. It is not that the old virtues are wrong, only wrongheaded; they no longer apply in the harsh, modern world. Their time was in the distant mythical America of small towns and enlightened leaders. This inadequacy is emphasized in the film by Derby's actions. For all his virtues, Derby is a curiously impotent father figure, ineffective in his ministrations to his children, and one who ultimately dies a victim of his own romantic conceptions. Nobody really listens to him, not Lazzaro, not the German commandant, nor the young German guard. Guided by archaic romantic ideals, Derby cannot fathom the nature of the American character. He cannot see, for example, that the savage energy of Lazzaro is just as much a part of America as the familial paradise from which he springs. Hill's camera, though, makes the point for the audience. In the election scene, Derby and Billy are foreground, Lazzaro in the rear, the composition of the shot reminding us that there is another dimension to be considered. In the letter scene, in which Derby talks of his love for his son, Lazzaro again lurks in the background, a silent counterpoint to the idealism of Derby and Billy. In addition to misjudging the Germans and Americans, Derby seems incapable of understanding the seriousness of his position. In one scene, for example, he and the other prisoners parade down a Dresden street; he and Billy talk, failing to see a corpse hanging in the background. The savagery of war is not visible to them, although the audience perceives it. Derby is forever distracted by the beauty of things, flowers and pieces of Dresden china. Though rare and admirable, this aesthetic sensibility leads to his senseless death.

Billy's simplistic idealism is shattered with Derby's death, and he is forced to seek some new vision, some new way of understanding the world. At first, as the shock treatment scenes make clear, he has difficulty in coping with his painful memories. But stability comes when he marries Val and lives as the archetypal middle-American burgher. Through the creation of a family unit and financial success he apparently hopes to overcome his sense of displacement and uneasiness. Yet his attempt fails. Billy is uncomfortable in Ilium, where his family is a travesty of the "nice" life recounted by Derby. Where Derby and his wife apparently loved and supported each other, Billy and his wife obviously do not. Where Derby and his son earned each other's respect, Billy and his son seem at odds. Robert is a vandal, an antisocial embarrassment, instead of a source of happiness. His metamorphosis into Green Beret and modern Howard Campbell, complete with "fag uniform" and anticommunist rhetoric, only exposes the magnitude of Billy's familial failure. His son falls by the wayside, betraying Billy like Val and Barbara. Uncomfortable in the father role, Billy compensates by the overwork that leads to his phenomenal material success and by a gift-giving habit that only highlights the emptiness of his relationships. His plane crash ends this particular segment of his life, revealing to him that transitory material things cannot provide the happiness he seeks. Val's death and Robert's transformation tear away the remaining illusions that Billy has foolishly entertained.

At this low point, Billy is suddenly whisked to Tralfamadore and given an opportunity to create the mythic American world that guaranteed happiness. He wins Montana, and with her begins the family unit he unsuccessfully searched for on earth. He and she share a love and a joy in their child that Billy never had with Val. As a bonus, Billy is also removed from the sufferings on Earth. Ilium and Dresden are just stations on a time-tripping journey, unpleasant moments that will ultimately be by-passed. The audience, which usually identifies with Billy, applauds his escape to the dome and Montana. Life on Tralfamadore seems an affirmation of the traditional American belief that those of good heart will eventually reap spiritual and emotional rewards.

But, as I also suggested earlier, this interpretation fails to account for the variations in the traditional genre story. Hill directs the broadly sketched characters and familiar plot in such a way that we

Billy Pilgrim and his two families: (top) in Ilium smiling with his father-in-law and wife (Sorrell Booke, Sharon Gans); (bottom) triumphant with Montana Wildhack (Valerie Perrine) on Tralfamadore.
(Credit: Movie Star News)

must question the simple view. Billy is transformed from naif to a spiritually enervated survivor of Dresden, a dreamer who uses the fantasy world of Tralfamadore as a shield against the suffering witnessed at Dresden. Consequently, Tralfamadore and the mythical American values associated with it become fantastical, their virtues inadequate and inappropriate for modern life.

The assertions of Billy and those of the Tralfamadorian voice make clear the true nature of the Tralfamadorian vision: on the planet there is no responsibility, suffering, or death. When Billy arrives in the dome, he is informed that there is no such thing as free will. "We've visited thirty-one inhabited planets," the voice tells him, "and studied reports of a hundred more. Only on earth is there talk of free will." Without free will, of course, there can be no individual responsibility, for actions are then determined by fate or chance. Better yet, Billy discovers, there is no time—everything has always been, is, and will be. Nor is there any pain. The soothing voice tells Billy that "the best way to spend a pleasant journey is to ignore the bad moments and concentrate on the good." Billy responds to this vision, and it has a miraculously salutary effect on him. In the final confrontation with his daughter and son-in-law, Billy makes it clear Tralfamadore has rescued him. "I'm not going to commit myself to an institution. If it weren't for Tralfamadore I might have needed an institution." For, as he says, "on Tralfamadore you learn that the world is just a collection of moments all strung together in beautiful random order." He has also learned that "if we're going to survive, it's up to us to concentrate on the good moments and ignore the bad." Billy has found a world which lacks individual responsibility, where suffering can be eliminated, and where death no longer limits. Even without Montana, Tralfamadore is a conventional paradise.

But the film undercuts Tralfamadore, just as it satirized Derby and Ilium. The style, structure, and content reveal that death, suffering, and accountability are integral parts of the universe; any attempt to deny their existence is a willful disregard of the facts, an unwarranted retreat into fantasy. Crucial to Billy's conception of the world is the idea of randomness, of moments strung together in arbitrary order. But the style of the film shows, contrary to his assertion, that all is interconnected. The events of the film are linked associatively, not in random order, suggesting that Billy's journey is internal, a mental exploration of his past and pondering of his future, not a real experience.

In the opening scene, for example, we go from the loud clicking of the typewriter to the clacking of the tanks, from the rasping sound of the slide into the foxhole back to the typewriter, from thoughts of Montana to Montana, and from a cooing Billy on Tralfamadore to a cooing Billy in the foxhole. The scenes are linked, not disparate. There are also other cuts that emphasize the connection between events. We move from the face in the soupbowl to the face on the lawn, the diamond in Derby's hand to the diamond at the anniversary party, and from the prisoner of war camp shower to the Ilium swimming pool shower. In addition, there are instances where two sequences are joined by a voice-over, a technique that creates an even stronger impression of unity. When selected from the prisoner of war line by the German photographer, Billy moves freely between his image and voice and that of the American photographer at the dedication of the Pilgrim building. On the operating table, Billy flashes back to Dresden, seeing incidents there, but hearing the respirator and the doctor's voice. Rumford's political tirade supports visuals from the hospital and Dresden, and the Tralfamadorian voice explains the dome and Dresden. After the operation, the Slaughterhouse-Five corridor dissolves into the Ilium hospital corridor, another transition device that links rather than separates the two incidents.[3]

Such devices disprove the randomness proclaimed by Billy, for they clearly join separate experiences. The transitions also show that the war is the dominant, formative experience in Billy's life, and suggest that we are witnessing an attempt to reconcile the past and the present. Almost all the cuts are between Dresden and some other segment of Billy's life. His trip up the stairs with Spot parallels his trip up the stairs of the bomb shelter; the flashing traffic light is intercut with the bombing of Dresden; the American photographer recalls the German; the plane crash throws him back to Dresden and Slaughterhouse-Five; the door to his room leads instead to the prisoner of war camp or to the annihilated city; and his son's call of "Dad" mingles with the young German's call of "Papa." He moves from the burning bodies in Dresden to Montana's arms; from the earth of Dresden to his couch on Tralfamadore; and from the roadway in Dresden to his final triumphant moment. Billy is still a prisoner of his war experiences, even on Tralfamadore.

If all is not random and arbitrary, beyond our control, then one may be able to make choices and be accountable for those choices. Free will is still a possibility. In addition, the film makes it clear, contrary to Billy's assertion, that time is an integral part of the universe. Billy blithely tells us he is free of time. The opening shots of the film show us an extreme close-up of Billy's letter to the Ilium paper: "I have become *unstuck in time*," he declares. Since his conversion to Tralfamadorianism, he is no longer bound by time, and can now travel freely between past, present, and future. As he tells his lecture audience, moments before his assassination by his old foe, Lazzaro, there is no mortality. "It's time for me to be dead for a little while, *and then live again.*" Resurrection is possible; life is eternal; man's age old dream of immortality has been attained. But the film questions this viewpoint. In the opening scene, before we meet Billy, we hear the ticking of a clock. As the camera moves through the house, viewing the world from his perspective, we hear the measured rhythm of the timepiece. The plane crash is preceded by the ubiquitous barbershop quartet, singing "there'll be some changes made," an ironic line, and an aural reminder for the audience that the world is fluid, not fixed. The operating room sequence is underpinned by the sound of the respirator, its regularity a mimic clock. In two crucial scenes the clock is an integral element, serving, when contrasted to Billy's Tralfamadorian dogma, to undercut his statements. The scene with Robert, the young Green Beret, is played against the sound of a ticking clock, even though such measured ticking would not be audible during an ordinary conversation. Robert's conversion to Campbellism is the final defeat for Billy. The father-son relationship so vital to Billy with his own father, with Derby, and now with Robert has been destroyed. The myth of the family, around which Billy has built his vision of happiness, is shattered, and the ticking of the clock places his loss in the stream of time, making it part of an ongoing process.

Later, after his election to and salvation on Tralfamadore, Billy returns to earth to defeat his nagging daughter. He calmly explains the paradise on Tralfamadore to her, apparently overcoming the interfering female presence at last. But ever present in the background is the ticking of a clock, one more reminder of a temporality Billy insists does not exist. Finally, the penultimate scene in the movie is built around the concept of time. Billy helps Lazzaro loot, appropriately enough, a grandfather clock, and he is soon pinned down by it when the others flee the sound of gunfire. The image, in conjunction with the other reminders of time, suggests Billy is *still* pinned by, and subordinate to time.

Billy's final claim that suffering can be eliminated is also questioned. First, we can note that an act of will abolishes suffering, a strange method for a planet without free will, and second that the narrative of the film makes Tralfamadore clearly escapist wish fulfillment. The dome serves as a refuge from, not an alternative to, Dresden and Ilium. Even though the events in the film are not chronological, there is still a definite narrative order. All crucial events occur within a short period of film time, and are so arranged that the pleasant ones seem a response to the painful. They are in effect intercut, and, as with all cross cutting, a relationship is established between the two incidents. For each failure he endures or pain he suffers, Billy is rewarded with a moment on Tralfamadore, and the conjunction suggests that Tralfamadore is an escape from the world.

The two climactic moments in his life, the experiences of Dresden and the devastation of life in Ilium, are joined by the mingling of the young German's cry of "Papa" and Robert's call of "Dad." They are followed by Billy's first trip to Tralfamadore. In his talk with the voice, Billy mentions Dresden, "the end of the world," and suddenly we are there, watching the collection and burning of the bodies. As Billy stands there, masked against the diseased air, watching the bodies of the women and children piled and burned, the voice tells him the way to spend a pleasant journey. Immediately Billy is back on Tralfamadore, encountering and winning Montana—an infinitely more pleasant experience than Dresden. Not only does the voice preach escapism, but the structure of the film suggests it. Billy's next visit to Dresden reveals the senseless death of Edgar Derby, but this is quickly overturned when we cut from Billy, slammed to the earth by the guards, to Billy recumbent on his couch in the dome, talking with Montana about having a baby. After the triumph over his daughter, his death scene, and the final experience in Dresden, Billy glances to the sky to catch sight of the sun. In the film, light has served as a metaphor for the avenue to Tralfamadore. At the sight of it, Billy finds himself once again in Montana's arms, a part of his family, at long last triumphantly attaining his ideals. Life in Ilium, Dresden, and even death have seemingly been overcome, but the triumph is muted for the audience by recognition of the narrative structure.

Tralfamadore is ultimately reduced to the status of a dream. The associative nature of Billy's "time-tripping" suggests his journey is mental, and thus Tralfamadore a mental way station, and the contravention of the Tralfamadorian vision also contributes to our perception of it as a mental phenomenon. The perceptive viewer realizes that Tralfamadore is an escapist fantasy.[4] Billy's idealistic beliefs have crumbled under the pressures of the world, and he has retreated inward to safety and security.

Our realization that Billy is deceiving himself reduces our sympathy for him. We discover that he is a dreamer, a child of fantasy whose purblind imagination has no resources other than fantasy (in this case Tralfamadore) for dealing with the horror and meaninglessness of modern life. We may sympathize with his problems, and even with him, but no longer identify with him because he and his solutions seem dwarfed by the complexity of the problems.

Billy's transformation from pleasant stereotype to complex character is effected through a variation of conventions and the use of motifs. First, we can note that Billy differs from the standard naive character. Ordinarily, characters in films of this genre demonstrate their right to their success by evidencing courage, pluck, some special skill, or just the ability to survive in a harsh world. Like Judy Holliday in *Born Yesterday*, the character should already possess the virtues and skills and only lack the opportunity or experience to use them. And usually the naive character wins some reconciliation with society, often through a romantic involvement with an acceptable member of society. Billy does none of these things. For all his good qualities, he demonstrates no special skill or virtue; he simply endures. Throughout the film he lacks the vitality, the distinguishing character, the enlightened but unarticulated wisdom, or the strength with which we can identify. Billy lacks character; as Rumford says, "I could carve a better man out of a banana." Nor does Billy triumph by virtue of his skill; he gains Tralfamadore and Montana accidentally. Nor does he effect a reconciliation with society. He attains his socially approved happiness in a world outside the recognizable social fabric.

In addition, Billy is presented as a child of fantasy, someone who understands the world in fairy-tale terms. He wears boots from the prisoner of war production of Cinderella, a story which deals with the kind of magical transformation Billy undergoes. He also talks of Dresden as "a land of Oz," and he later tells Val "to follow the yellow brick road," the ribbon, to the car. The story of Oz, with its emphasis on the permanent and abiding virtues of the honest family, also has special relevance for Billy's story. His entrance into Dresden shows him as a pied piper, a child among children, oblivious to the concerns of the war. Adult fantasies are also a part of his life, as the longing looks at the whores suggest. The drive-in scene with the Montana porn film shows the same sexual fantasies. As the nude princess calls to her attendant, Billy wishfully nods yes, yes to the voice.

Billy's escapist vision is further emphasized by the blanket motif. We see him wrap himself in a blanket for protection from the physically and psychically unpleasant. It surrounds him as he stumbles through the snow, and later as he trudges in the prisoner of war line. When the old timer in the box car begins talking about the hard winters in Troy (which is the Anglicization of Ilium), Billy draws the blanket over his head. We then cut to the hospital where Billy, crablike, peers out of the blanket at his mother and Mr. Rosewater. The way he shuts out his mother is emblematic of the way Billy eventually shuts out all painful experiences. But the futility of such action is illustrated in the second box-car scene. Weary rips off the blanket to accuse Billy of murder, forcing Billy to witness his death.

A more telling demonstration of Billy's limitations is Hill's use of light. It serves as the medium by which Billy ascends to Tralfamadore, and thus it becomes a visual metaphor for Tralfamadore. Light's long association with poetic inspiration may also be operating here, and Billy's ability to accept and incorporate Tralfamadore is evidence of his open imagination. However, in the film light also reveals not only the familial paradise of Tralfamadore, but also the grotesque world of Dresden and the war, the symbol of death and horror here on earth. Billy's positive use of light contrasts with the more negative use made of it in the film, and the discrepancy again suggests that Billy is myopic, that his vision is selective.

In the world of the film, light reveals more than happiness. In the box car, the German guard's weaving flashlight intermittently reveals Weary's frozen face. The searchlights in the prisoner of war camp illuminate not only the singing, vivacious British, but the brutish Russians as well. The composition of the shots of the two groups is similar; light above and behind illuminates both Russians and the cheerful welcoming party of the British. Later the blinking, shaking light of the bomb shelter creates a pattern that matches that of the incendiary bombs walking across Dresden, and that in turn is inter-cut with the blinking red traffic light. Light thus triggers associations with Dresden as well as Tralfamadore. When candles are lit in the bomb shelter, the bottom lighting creates grotesque shadows; the German commandant's head, for example, becomes a death mask. And the movement from the protective dark of the shelter to the light of day and the annihilated city typifies the relationship between light and dark in the film. The former is a source of pain, the latter protects from harm.

Even the Tralfamadorian light is associated with death. Its first appearance coincides with Billy's eviction from his son's christening party. As the song in the background ironically proclaims "true love will come shining through," Billy sits despondently on the lawn. The Tralfamadorian light comes down, shines briefly, and disappears. Billy follows it into the sky. The camera rests on the sky briefly and momentarily we hear Lazzarro's voice, once again threatening Billy. The point seems clear: The same sky which houses Tralfamadore houses Lazarro. Later, on Tralfamadore, Billy and Montana will ask for the night canopy so that they can get acquainted. The camera pulls back to reveal the dome against the heavens, then pans right, the stars gradually dissolving into the reflections from the Dresden china figurine in Derby's hand. Once again the film suggests that Dresden and Tralfamadore are a continuum, not separate entities, and that Billy has selectively chosen those elements he wishes to see.

Billy Pilgrim, then, fails to be the classic American hero. His voyage is not one outward to discovery, but inward to fantasy. He creates a vision of happiness that protects more than Derby's idealism or Val's materialism; divorced from reality, it protects him from reality. Fantasies are not necessarily harmful or escapist, but Billy's is obviously a retreat from the problems created by his wartime experiences.

The film questions the dream and the dreamer, and thus asks that we examine the values associated with the fantasy world. It offers no solutions of its own to the problems that defeat Billy, and perhaps that is a major fault, but it suggests that the spiritual homilies we take for granted—the exaltation of family and virtue—are insufficient also and in need of revision. Through its ironic mode, the film makes the discovery of the limitation of traditional beliefs seem our own, and its point is made more forcefully than something didactic like *Johnny Got His Gun*. No longer will the audience be allowed, as Billy suggests, "to ignore the bad moments and concentrate on the good."

Slaughterhouse-Five shows one man's, an Everyman's, inability to cope with the complexities and difficulties of modern life.[5] And, like *Butch Cassidy*, it lays the blame for this problem on the antiquated assumptions of the culture. The examination of the cultural conventions, however, is far from complete, for Hill, in his next film, continues to explore, again through genre, the American social fabric.

4

The Sting

IT WOULD SEEM a contravention of both critical and popular taste to assert that *The Sting* (1973), Hill's most commercially successful film, is more than simple entertainment. Yet it is possible to see the film not only as a genre study, another intelligent and wryly ironic dissection of our culture, but also as evidence of Hill's continued artistic growth. For the first time in his career, Hill examines film as a medium of expression, including the aesthetic conventions associated with the traditional genre films; more importantly, he uses that examination to offer an alternative to the thought crystallized in those outworn conventions.

If viewed as a double narrative, a genre story with carefully wrought variations, *The Sting* can be seen as an attack on the sacred cultural tenets of individualism, success, and the certainty of justice. The two con men are typical Hollywood protagonists: individuals distinguished from the mass of men by their intelligence, skills, and fortitude. Not only are they types with whom the audience can identify, but their actions confirm some traditional American cultural notions. In realizing their revenge, they show, first, that the world (represented in this case by the Coleman family and the community of "good" con men) is best served by strong individuals with the strength and courage to stand up to large, impersonal forces; second, that our traditional scheme of justice is still valid, and that there are no people above or beyond the law; and third, that success belongs primarily to the individual of uncommon skill (not organization men like Lonnegan) who exerts uncommon effort.

While these recognizable ideas are obviously at work in the film, they are not the sum and total of *The Sting*. Once again there are significant variations in the development of the story and an ambigu-

59

ous conclusion that work to undercut the expected response. The con men are shown to share some of Lonnegan's distasteful qualities, and this blurs the distinction from the ordinary that they claim for themselves. Their excessive reliance on self leads to as many problems as it does solutions, suggesting that the concept of individuality is not as liberating and untroubled as they believe. They do not achieve the justice they seek, and, after realizing this fact, are not particularly concerned; they seem content with the pleasure they have had pulling off the sting. The discrepancy between the expected and the actual conclusions forces the viewer to reexamine the film and the conventions, such as individuality, the desirability of success, or appropriate justice—almost givens in American cinema—upon which it is based.

In addition, Hill uses the story, with its detailing of an elaborate ruse, to fashion a reflexive work that comments on the nature of film. The con men are artist figures, and their actions closely parallel those of a director making a film. However, with the ambiguous results of their production, they are, more properly, examples of how not to create, and the counterpoint between their work and Hill's film focuses our attention on the issues involved in creative work.

Such an interpretation admittedly flies in the face of accepted critical opinion. Most critics, while admitting the film's commercial potential, dismissed it. Pauline Kael, who led the onslaught, is typical in her remarks.

The Sting . . . is meant to be roguishly charming entertainment, and I guess that's how most of the audience takes it, but I found it visually claustrophobic, and totally mechanical. It keeps cranking on, section after section, and it doesn't have a good spirit . . . the director is the implacably impersonal George Roy Hill. The script, by David S. Ward, is a collection of Damon Runyon hand-me-downs with the flavor gone.[1]

Paul Zimmerman of *Newsweek* found it enjoyable, but stale, light entertainment.[2] Stanley Kauffmann and Colin Westerbeck concurred, with only John Simon giving unqualified approval.[3] No serious film journal bothered with a review, but some critics did find it more than mechanical. Stanley Solomon, in *Beyond Formula,* saw it as a well-done and enjoyable variation of the crime film.[4]

One can, however, move past these cursory judgments by noting the ways in which the film fulfills and then diverges from the genre requirements. As Stuart Kaminsky notes, *The Sting* is a big caper film, a member of a genre that has a conflict between individuals and an impersonal society, a concentration on an elaborate scheme to steal massive amounts of money, a requirement of great skill to achieve the goal, an understandable and sympathetic reason for the commission of the crime, and success.[5] Hill's story meets all these criteria. The two distinct individuals, Hooker and Gondorff, work against a heartless organization, represented by Doyle Lonnegan; their elaborate scheme requires great skill; and the audience emotionally endorses the con artists, not only because they are more human and engaging than Lonnegan, but also because their motive—revenge—is understandable and sympathetic in the context of the film. And, of course, they succeed. Stanley Solomon asserts that the crime film must establish a moral hierarchy, with some criminals more sympathetic than the others; work with a plot that requires great skill; give an understandable motive to the protagonists; and grant them success. *The Sting* also meets his genre criteria, for it, as Solomon notes, "provides a brilliant example of how the genre creates a reasonable facsimile of moral order within a situation that in a real-life equivalent would be beyond moral considerations." As Solomon sees it, "Redford's motivation is revenge against the man who ordered his colleague's murder." In spite of the complex plot, "the overriding issue is clear; Redford and Newman risk their lives to pull off their confidence game, not for the huge sums of money they can gain from it but, on Newman's part, for the sake of the artistry of his plan and his affection for Redford and, on Redford's part, out of a desire to revenge his murdered friend."[6]

The most important point in this big caper film, for both Kaminsky and Solomon, is motive, and this essential characteristic deserves some elaboration. The con men gain our sympathy because their desire to avenge Luther's death implicitly affirms a concept central to the American understanding of the world. The idea of justice, a moral-legal system that operates to reward right and punish wrong, is ingrained in most Americans, who are taught from childhood that those who transgress are punished, certainly in the afterlife and usually in this life. The concept places evil in perspective, and comfortingly assures believers of the eventual triumph of a just, benevolent world. For most viewers, the con artist's revenge is not pointless, irrational vengeance but rather a just punishment of a criminal beyond the law. This conventional precept forms the base upon which *The Sting* is built.

The other key elements in the con men's attraction for the viewer are their individuality and their attainment of success. American audiences have always identified with characters who stand apart from and above the social group, and who, by virtue of their difference, succeed in realizing goals past the reach of the average man. Such characters affirm the values of the social group (since they are its most advanced form of expression) and their success serves as testimony that the group's dreams, such as an orderly, comprehensible world, are indeed attainable. The con men are by definition outside society and the law, though they retain strong affection for the ordinary people in their world. They not only take pride in their difference, but also in the fact that their success is a result of their own efforts. They do not bully people (as does Lieutenant Snyder), play dirty or cheat (as does Lonnegan), or prey on the innocent; they succeed because they are skilled, independent operators who exert control over their lives and their environment. While they use their skills for personal gain, they remain attractive because they are willing to protect those less resourceful than themselves and maintain some semblance of a moral order. Most importantly, though, they appear to succeed; their actions resolve the tensions and unfairness of the situation and give both the individuals and the group satisfaction. Like the Westerner or the private eye, the con men implicitly tell us that success and social order are rooted in the strong individual and the simple code of ethics.

Not only are the characters and their attitudes familiar, but *The Sting* is also reassuring to a general audience from an aesthetic standpoint. It harks back to the golden age of movies when films were entertainment, free from such problems as narrative discontinuity, concentration on the distasteful, pessimism, or obscurity. Then, audience and film industry seemed in agreement on the purpose and content of films, and the escapist fare celebrating chamber of commerce virtues was satisfying to both parties. With its stylized production, *The Sting* seems to deliberately recall the films of the 1930s, and its plot, so relentlessly ingenious, prevents contemplation of any issues. As most critics commented, the film was a paradigm of pure entertainment.

Hill undercuts this apparently seamless genre piece by encouraging a questioning of the genre conventions and characters. By presenting the film as a work structured for a purpose, and by defusing the commercial illusion that we are watching a self-contained, complete world, Hill stimulates a critical, distanced attitude that moves us beyond the stock response to genre films.[7] Attention focused on the artifice prevents attention to the characters, and the distance that results makes it easier and more natural to question both them and their motives.

The opening and closing titles serve as a frame which calls attention to the role of manipulation in the film. Drawn in the *Saturday Evening Post* style associated with the thirties, the titles seem a calculated commercial ploy, but four of the five (the first is the only exception) make some indirect reference to the film as constructed work. The second shows the characters in costume on a set, with director Hill looking on from the left; the third, writer Ward looking on another set from the right; and the fourth, the two masks that are the traditional symbols of performance. The ending title shows workers dismantling the wire-shop props, another reminder of the structured nature of the film. Significantly, this is preceded by a momentary break between the final iris-out and the last title during which we hear Marvin Hamlisch's voice counting out the beat for the musicians. The obvious deliberateness of the break and the subject of the final title bring us back to the starting point: What we have watched was put together, and we are meant to note its constructed nature. Within the film proper, the wipes and irises contribute to our consciousness of artifice. By their very nature, these devices, rejected by most filmmakers because of their obviousness, call attention to the *making* involved in filmmaking.

The story also contains several incidents that contribute to the distancing effect suggested by the titles and transitional devices. By emphasizing that appearance is manipulative, the scenes implicitly ask us to step back and examine the phenomenological world more carefully. The two biggest surprises in the film, for most, are the revelations of the Sallino and FBI subplots. Each works because the audience brings stock expectations to the incidents. Most assume that Loretta is the love-interest; she seems honest and lonely, and aids Hooker in his escape from the gunman. Our attention is focused on the black-gloved man who, with his stylized dress and Italian features, seems a more conventional threat. Such judgment causes a reversal of expectations in the alley gunfight that, while in one way a source of pleasure, serves as an implicit reminder of the inadequacy of stock responses. The "death" scene is even more of a surprise because once again the audience accepts conventions so unhesitatingly. The deaths of Cole and Sallino are filmed in the traditional Hollywood stylized manner, with bright red aniline dye and no excessive gore. The final scene is shot in exactly the same way, and we assume the characters are dead. When they pop back to life, we cheer, because the surprise makes the Mick's loss more complete. But the reversal of expectations, forgotten in the triumph, is equally important. By playing with accepted conventions, conventions that the film itself uses in earlier scenes, Hill calls attention to the artificiality of the surface, pointing out that anything can be manipulated for effect.

In addition, the film as a whole can be seen as a series of incidents structured for effect. We are continually confronted with scenes in which appearances have been manipulated, and these scenes provide not only entertainment (because we usually are aware of the manipulation), but, when taken as a group, remind us of the illusory nature of any surface—including, by extension, the film itself. The opening scene shows the numbers operation delayed by a "raid" meant to keep up the mayor's reputation for honesty. The first con involves an attempt by the numbers runner to trick the two men (he promises them their money will be safe with him) as well as the con of the numbers runner by the grifters. We also witness the crooked gambling den in which Hooker loses his money; the counterfeit money that buys time from Lieutenant Snyder; Hooker's cheery disposition, which masks his despair at losing the money, and his calm acquiescence, which masks his anger at Luther's retirement; Hooker's continued silence about the pursuit of the thugs and Snyder; the transformation of Hooker into "Kelly"; the refined surface that hides Lonnegan's crudity; Lonnegan's attempted con of "Shaw"; Loretta Sallino's performance; the revelation of the black-gloved man's purpose; the Western Union ploy; all the action in the wire-shop; the FBI drama enacted for Snyder; and, of course, the "death" scene. In every sequence we discover that there is an additional dimension to the situation which, when perceived, alters our understanding of it. The characters (and occasionally the audience) are deceived only because they bring certain assumptions to the incidents instead of relying on objective evidence and their own intelligence.

The critical attitude encouraged by the titles, transitional devices, and the story makes us sensitive to the ways in which the characters differ from the usual genre figures. The first significant variation is the linkage of the con men to Lonnegan. We gradually discover that there are similarities between the two groups, and this prevents the total sympathetic identification common in most films of the genre.[8] Lonnegan and Gondorff, for example, despite their obvious differences in personality, characteristics, and goals, share a number of traits. Both men are directors of organizations, and both use their subordinates to further their own goals. In the card-game sequence, both men are performing. Lonnegan, crude, emotional, and vicious, hides behind a mask of refinement and rationality; Gondorff hides his

The manipulation of appearances during the key operation in The Sting.
(Courtesy: Museum of Modern Art/Film Stills Archive)

intelligence behind a facade of vulgarity and simplicity, playing the
fool for others. Both men cheat, but neither for monetary gain.
Lonnegan wants "to bust that bastard bookie once and for all";
Gondorff must prod Lonnegan into revenge. Obviously, the central
action of the picture, the unfolding of the sting, involves both men in
the same sort of role playing. Lonnegan pretends to be a bettor,
Gordorff a bookie; Lonnegan wants to revenge and enrich himself,
while Gondorff wants revenge and the pleasure of seeing his plan
work. Both are masters of illusion who recognize the importance of
facade. Lonnegan tells Floyd he must kill in order to preserve his
image of strength, to keep others from testing him. Gondorff tells
Hooker that "you've got to keep his [Lonnegan's] con after you take
his money"; the illusion must be maintained to forestall revenge. And
both are willing to play rough to maintain their facades. Lonnegan has
his men kill Luther so that the illusion of omnipotence can be kept;
Gondorff has his friend protect Hooker by killing Sallino, again in
order to protect the illusion of the wire-store. The fact that neither
man pulls the trigger does not mitigate their responsibility for the
killings; nor does the fact that the action is directed against criminals
alter the immorality of the act.[9] We excuse the con men because their
motives seem to justify such actions, but later even this judgment
must be altered.

Hill also uses editing and composition to suggest a union between
the two groups. Several match cuts throughout the film join the
movement of members of both groups. For example, after Hooker
loses his money and his date, he moves right to left down a street; the
picture then wipes to a car moving right to left toward Lonnegan's
headquarters. Shortly thereafter we cut from Floyd moving right to
left away from Lonnegan to Hooker moving right to left up the stairs
to Luther's. The transition between the golf course scene and the first
merry-go-round scene is made with a reverse spin that joins the
motions of Floyd and Gondorff. Later there will be similar reverse
spins that move us from Hooker's face outside the wire-shop to
Loretta's at the cafe, and Snyder's visage in the FBI headquarters to
Gondorff's in the brothel room. Such transitions subtly suggest a
union between two worlds that convention demands be kept
separate.

Lighting and composition also associate the con men with Lonnegan. For example, there is a strong vertical line motif used in connection with both. The opening shot follows Mottola up the stairs, the

vertical motion joined with the horizontal lines of the steps. Immediately after the first con, Hooker and Luther are associated with vertical lines, which, with their connotation of prison, suggest criminal activity. They are framed through a gate with vertical slats, and run through it, pausing in the vertical shadows. The window just behind Hooker is blocked with vertical bars. After they split, Hooker is seen through the vertical bars of the pawn shop, buying the egregiously garish suit. On three separate occasions, high angle shots of Hooker entering an apartment building are framed through the vertical slats of the banisters. Also, the vertical lines created by the merry-go-round poles adumbrate this compositional device, as does the vertical movement of the freight elevator in Lonnegan's packing house (as a freight elevator, it is constructed of vertical slats) and Hooker's ascension in the hotel elevator. Lonnegan is framed by the vertical bars of the cashier's cage, and for a moment Gondorff stands beside him, also framed by the bars of an adjoining cage. The vertical motif, with its suggestion of prison strongest in this shot, makes the two leaders seem well-dressed prisoners in adjacent cells.

A horizontal line motif is just as strong. Almost all the interiors in the film seem shaded by Venetian blinds, and the light filtering through them casts a shadow which again reminds one of prison. The room in Lonnegan's packing house is shuttered with blinds, and as he stands in the gloom the light casts horizontal shadows across his chest. Gondorff's office is similarly enclosed, establishing yet another link between him and Lonnegan, and he is seen as a shadow behind the blinds. Hooker, just before he leaves the diner, is also bathed in the horizontal shadow of its blinds. The similarity of the lines seems intended to connect all three men, particularly when the unnatural lighting of these situations is considered. Lonnegan stands facing a wall, but the blinds still somehow cast a shadow; Hooker faces an empty, windowless counter, yet again there are shadows falling across his chest.

The suggestion of union beneath the surface is a significant variation of the genre conventions, but the greatest difference between the characters and our expectations of them involves their motive. The importance of motive has already been discussed; it is essentially the justification for their actions. We pardon their immorality, such as cheating in the card game or murdering Sallino, because the revenge motive is a sympathetic one. However, as the picture progresses, we discover that the con artists are driven as much by self-interest as revenge, and that they have only a minimal commitment to the concept of justice. This revelation alters our understanding of them and their actions, and questions their role as unqualified heroes.

Most critics and viewers assume the con men are motivated by revenge. Solomon is typical when he says "Redford's motivation is revenge against the man who ordered his colleague's murder . . . the overriding issue is clear."[10] But contrary to that statement and the general belief, the primary stimulus is self-gratification. The sting serves as an opportunity for Gondorff to prove himself, just as crime serves as an opportunity for Butch and Sundance to prove themselves and the battle with Kessler as an opportunity for Waldo to prove himself. Through the successful perpetration of a crime, Gondorff defines himself as an individual; the success gives him a sense of identity. The fact is not revealed until late in the film, until we have already committed our sympathies to the con men, but it cannot be ignored. Gondorff implicitly tells Hooker that he was never interested in money or security. He had those years ago when he worked with a mob that fleeced with impunity, but did not like the benefits. "No use being a grifter if it's the same as being a citizen." Gondorff is an artist who cons to show his skill, to exercise his virtuosity. Apparently the pleasure of proving himself a successful, distinct individual motivates him, and this motivation is eventually conveyed to Hooker.

Originally Hooker shared that view. We remember his comments to Erie that he "likes grifting" and has no intention of settling down or realizing any gain. However, Luther's death has pushed him away from his self-interest; he now wants a just vengeance against Lonnegan, and he lets his emotional commitment to that drive him. He is so intent on revenge that he does not listen carefully to what Gondorff has to say. In the first meeting between the two men, Gondorff intimates that vengeance (justice) is not possible. The master con man is reluctant to take on Hooker because he does not "want no hot-head looking to get even coming back halfway through saying it [the con] ain't enough [to avenge Luther]—because it's all we're going to get." Hooker overlooks that remark, even though his actions indicate that he senses Gondorff's lack of commitment to the principles of vengeance. He refuses to tell his friends about the pursuit of Lieutenant Snyder or Lonnegan's torpedoes because he is afraid that Gondorff will, as he promised, "fold the con" should the danger become too great. This indirectly shows that Gondorff does not believe in a quid-pro-quo system of justice, and that he would move on, without revenging Luther, with no regrets. Later, in a crucial scene in Gondorff's room, the older man makes his point explicit. Hooker apologizes for the danger, saying he would not ask such a sacrifice except for Luther. But Gondorff flatly states that he is not doing it for Luther: "*Revenge is for suckers*; I've been grifting for thirty years and I never got any." Asked why he is doing it, he shrugs: "It seems worthwhile, doesn't it?" Hooker again overlooks the remarks, perhaps because he does not understand them, but finally comes around to Gondorff's point of view. After succumbing to his emotions and spending the night with the waitress, he seems to undergo a metamorphosis after her attempt on his life. He returns to the wire-shop and exchanges a glance with Gondorff, a tacit indication that he has learned his lesson. The two men have reached an understanding. "You're right," Hooker says at the end, "*it's not enough—but it's awfully close.*" It satisfies his urge for revenge, even though he now realizes that a simple, appropriate punishment will never be possible.

What we see, then, is an admission by both men that there can be no revenge and, by extension, no justice. They have no belief in any ordering force or that right will punish and balance wrong. Instead, they realize that the experience itself is its own reward and success proof of one's existence and identity. The refusal to take the money is not one last magnanimous gesture, but a measure of the con men's commitment to the principle of self. Knowing that they have succeeded is a much greater reward than money or the satisfaction of revenge. The motive, then, is a combination of revenge and self-interest, with the accent on the latter.

The characters in *The Sting* are thus substantially different from the prototypical genre figures, and their novel motivation frustrates the conventional conclusions. Justice is not truly effected (Lonnegan does not know that he has been "punished" for Luther's death), and the con men recognize that Hooker's moral code no longer applies, even if the audience does not. Instead of despairing, they are not particularly concerned. Seemingly more in tune with Lonnegan's theory of might makes right, they are satisfied with the pleasure of perpetrating the sting and look forward to another adventure. Concern for others, one of the major reasons they appeal to the audience, has evaporated and been replaced by a focus on the self.

This turning away from the social group is the primary indication that their doctrine of individuality, another major reason for their appeal, has failed them. Separateness from the common (those incapable of carrying out the sting) is traditionally a source of strength, but here it is a form of weakness. The con men have closed off the world to the point that they are isolated from it, trapped in an almost solipsistic universe. This estrangement is suggested in the setting, which admits no other social group (the Western Union manager is the only normal character), and the composition of many shots. Almost all the sets are closed, confined spaces (the train, the carousel, the small rooms in the whorehouse, the wire-shop, the alleys), color has developed into muted greens and browns, and the characters are often framed behind bars, or shades, or slats, or framed through doorways, hallways, or window frames to suggest confinement. They have become, Hill's camera suggests, trapped in that world, and their separateness, which supposedly frees them from the limitations of the group, has become restrictive.

The enervating nature of the individuality is clearly indicated in the relationship between Gondorff and Hooker. The older man is obviously a teacher, transforming a diamond in the rough into a master con man, changing both his appearance and his ways of thinking. While Hooker's physical change is clear—the tousled hair and garish suits give way to polished elegance—the mental transformation is both less obvious and less pleasing. Hooker begins, as noted earlier, fired by his simple scheme of justice: he believes in fair play, standing up for his friends, and enforcing the unwritten laws of his code, as is demonstrated by his actions at the crooked roulette game and his concern for Luther. This awareness of and concern for others is also evidenced in his need to establish a relationship with someone. While not the most discerning of men, Hooker's attempt to court the waitress testifies to his need for companionship.

Yet Hooker eventually gives us his old notions. Gondorff's repeated sermons about the futility of revenge finally make an impression, and the older man's more selfish view becomes ascendant. This is clearly indicated in the scene in Gondorff's room, when Henry declares that "revenge is for suckers." As Gondorff talks, the camera moves behind his head, and an unusual, unbalanced composition results. Gondorff's head occupies the whole right half of the screen, while Hooker is seen on the left, farther away, smaller, and trapped between the huge head and the wall. But the epiphany does not come until after Hooker's near fatal encounter with Loretta Sallino. Only then, as his exchange of glances with Gondorff indicates, does he realize that entanglements with others can be dangerous and that self-interest is primary.

The Sting, then, shows Hooker's progress from a traditional form of individuality, where individuals sought the group's greater good, to a more modern form which defines success as self-satisfaction. The old ideal has been perverted and the new result is less appealing and, unfortunately, far more common. In conjunction with the failure to achieve justice, this warped form of individuality effectively negates any feelings we may have for the con men, and turns our attention to the precepts which inform their adventure.

In addition to examining the genre's metaphysics Hill also examines its aesthetic conventions. The emphasis on artifice and the manipulable surface not only distances us from the characters, but reminds us that we are watching a film, a particular form of artifice. The same questioning attitude applied to the medium as well as the genre content reveals differences between Hill's film and some of the tacit aesthetic assumptions of the conventional film. Where the traditional film is secure in its assumptions, *The Sting* is questioning; where the earlier films serve as a pleasant form of escape, requiring only passive attention, Hill's film stimulates viewer participation; and where older films reassure through the retelling of a familiar narrative, *The Sting* discomforts through variations on the familiar. The true genre film, in enshrining society's idealized conventions, provides a refuge from thought about society's inconsistencies, flaws, or problems. *The Sting,* by urging us to examine the accepted conventions, initiates a dialogue on them. The one set of films follows an aesthetic which demands of the filmmaker invisibility, illusion, and pleasure—an artificer who delights. Hill shows that instead the filmmaker can use artifice to question his material, his world, and even the purpose and nature of his work.

A second reflexive element in *The Sting* is the resemblance between the characters' performance for Lonnegan and the making of a film. The crime/performance parallel is developed slowly as *The Sting* unfolds. There is the preproduction meeting between Gondorff and his associates, the discussion of a suitable script, the carefully planned card game and the attendant leg work that can be considered as the preproduction work, the renting of a location and props, the creation of a set, the hiring and costuming of extras, characters applying makeup, small scenes played out, rewriting to meet contingencies, the extras waiting to go on, special effects (the blanks and the blood capsules), the striking of the set, and the final payoff.

A comparison, however, emphasizes the differences between *The Sting* and the film-within-the-film. While the con men are ingenious, they are also trapped by a smugness and a lack of self-awareness. The certainty that they are right, and that all their actions can be excused by the momentousness of their goal, informs their art as well as their activities. Their only questions are questions of utility: what will work in the con of Lonnegan? They never ask if their actions have any significance beyond the phenomenological, or if there is anything they can learn about themselves from their actions. The primary concern is the gratification they can receive, not any consideration of the additional effects that pleasure may have for them. Such an art is dead. In its insistence on a perfected illusion that brings pleasure, their art is limited and unrewarding. They play a variation of the same basic scenario each time; the only variable is success, which is but a transitory satisfaction. There is nothing novel in the situation: they do not change, their audience (Lonnegan) does not change, and there is no consideration of the larger world since that would lessen the pleasure of the game.

In contrast, Hill uses film to question his subjects and to examine the nature of his chosen medium. Rather than take his world for granted, he uses artifice to call attention to the material of illusion, and suggests that the pleasing primary colors of traditional narrative are tainted. Hill assumes an audience interested in the subjects of his films, and rejects self-contained, escapist fare put on for the digestion of a passive audience. There is a concern with society and with film, and his ironic questioning style argues for a more responsive, open, socially conscious filmmaking. As his film demonstrates, the artist must go beyond familiar limits to achieve anything of value.

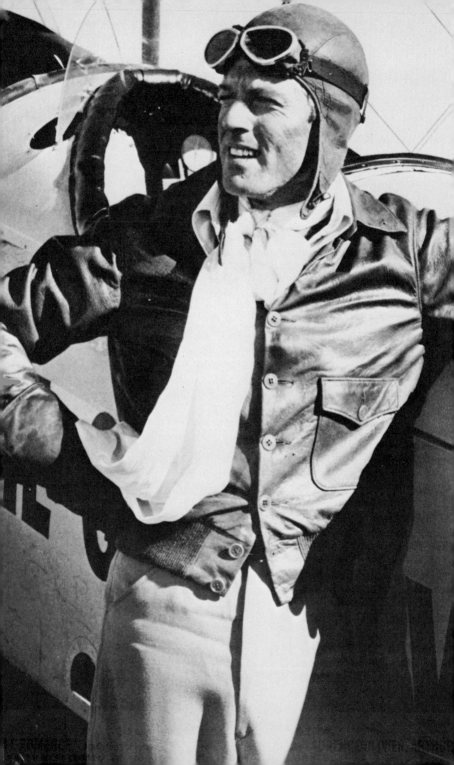

5

The Great Waldo Pepper

THE GREAT WALDO PEPPER (1976) was both a critical and a commercial failure, dismissed by reviewers as a clichéd melodrama and rejected by audiences who found its abrupt shifts in mood unsettling. The film, a personal project of Hill's (long an aviation buff), sought to capture the excitement of the early days of flying and to suggest the daredevil pilot's singular state of mind. But the subject, some stale narrative action, and, perhaps, Hill's closeness to the material worked against the creation of another popular success. *The Sting* and *Butch Cassidy* dealt with subjects which, although situated in the past, were still part of the American filmgoing public's consciousness; cowboys and gangsters, in their various permutations, have long been magnets for moviegoers. In addition, the narratives associated with these genres are so ingrained that the audience can anticipate the story or enjoy the way the film plays with traditions.

With *Waldo Pepper*, the audience was not on familiar ground. Although the daredevil exploits of aviators may have once attracted the public, the relationship long ago tapered off into something tenuous. The coming of the jet age depersonalized pilots to the point that their lives have no more built-in interest than, say, the lives of professional bowlers. Films with fliers as heroes all but disappeared from the popular cinema, and there are few familiar materials with which a filmmaker may work. Successful treatment of such a subject demands a blending of the most basic of Hollywood's adventure/ romance conventions, and yet it is, surprisingly, in this area that Hill's film has several weaknesses.

The central character is different from both Hollywood heroes and antiheroes, and his actions seem to repulse viewers rather than attract them. Waldo performs very few heroic deeds, passes his great test seemingly through the agency of chance instead of his own efforts, and lacks such important character attributes as great intelligence, probity, or strength. The sudden, capricious shifts in mood, from light comedy to melodrama to gruesome action, also tend to alienate the audience. Mary Beth's fall and Ezra's death are alien to the tenor of adventure films, not only because they are unexpected and brutal, but because they are pointless. Neither incident seems to help Waldo in his quest for perfection, and their inclusion causes a disorientation in the audience that is never relieved. The scenes are such obvious variations on conventional actions that they seem more suitable to Robert Altman than Hill, and their coexistence with some of the more traditional sequences results in a hybrid that pleases neither old nor new audiences.

Despite all these problems, *Waldo Pepper* is, as are all Hill's productions, more than just another typical genre film, and it has strong and rewarding elements to recommend it. Through it, Hill continues his study of the American concept of heroism and he also explores the nature of film, a subject that he first introduced in *The Sting*. Hill's treatment of these subjects is more complex and stimulating than in the earlier works, a sign that he is continuing to develop as an artist rather than simply restate old positions.

Individualism and heroism, the intertwined concepts that have absorbed so much of the American audience's attention and energy, are here given shadings missing from Hill's earlier studies. In previous films, the various facets of individualism were shown to be hollow, as in *Slaughterhouse-Five*, or outmoded, as in *Butch Cassidy*. In this film, the dreams which motivate Waldo are shown to have a value missing from, and perhaps preferable to, the world Waldo inhabits. The concept of individualism is no longer presented as an enervating, blinding social legacy, but as a tangible and once valuable part of our culture. Further, Waldo at least reaches an understanding of his situation, of his relationship with the "ordinary" world, that was denied to earlier Hill protagonists. He recognizes that he must choose between his ideals of heroism and living in a world that only pays lip service to those ideals.

Film and popular culture do not fare as well; they are shown as distorting lenses which not only alter the truth about our cultural experiences, but also, in their indifference to the experience, in their simple-minded striving to gain our attention, have vitiated the inherent strengths of the medium. Film, as presented in *Waldo Pepper*, is used to manipulate an audience, not to encourage it to experience or understand a subject, and the result is a medium remarkable for the

shallowness of its ideas and the feebleness of its product. In opposition to this type of film, Hill urges a more independent cinema that
involves the audience and appeals to its intelligence. By contrasting
the ways in which several artists work (Waldo, Dillhoefer, Werfel)
and the results obtained from their different approaches, Hill shows
that art can be a liberating experience that brings the world into a
sharper focus, and not just an appeal to the visceral emotions.

In developing these two major themes, Hill relies on his narrative
and on variations on the traditional narrative structures; the primary
difference between this film and other Hill works is that the genre
narrative is as important to the development of the themes as are the
variations. The discussion of ideas begins in the pretitle sequence.
We are shown a series of still photographs, alternately encountering a
pilot striking a gallant pose and then a crashed plane. The dates of
birth and death beneath the photos suggest a brief, violent life; the
contrasting images, a simple bit of parallel editing, hint at a negative
side to the heroic pose adopted by the young pilots, implying an
inevitable end to their brief transit. Although only suggested, not
stated, the concept of heroism is here given a shading often missing
from more traditional genre features.

The story proper, while superficially familiar, begins to develop
the idea sketched in the pretitle sequence. The first portion of the
film, detailing Waldo's exploits as a barnstorming pilot, is the most
traditional part of the narrative. In it we have clearly presented the
notion of the hero as a gifted individual who enjoys success and
esteem as a natural consequence of his skills. The characters are
storybook America, hardworking farmers and talented native sons,
sharing the pastoral simplicity of rural life. Waldo is a genial huckster,
selling rides, and an authentic hero with a tale of an encounter with
the legendary Ernst Kessler. More, he is a hero with a quest; he
wants to be the best pilot in the world, and the film will apparently be
a detailing of Waldo's climb to that pinnacle.

Most critics took this sequence as typical of the film, usually
excoriating the movie for its simple-mindedness.[1] The Norman
Rockwell America seemed too pat, with ideas and characters belong-
ing to a world, both real and cinematic, that was left behind long ago.
However, contrary to the reviewers' assertions, the sequence is
atypical in the narrative. That day in the country is the dream Waldo
aspires to: a place where his exploits have earned him the hero's just
rewards. But, as Waldo admits, such days and places are increasingly
rare, and the film, rather than repeating the expected dream, chroni-

cles instead Waldo's futile attempts to recapture that dream existence.

The sequence at the farm also involves the first of many performances, and this one, Waldo's tale at the dinner table, is, like his golden day, archetypal in its perfection. As a storyteller, Waldo shares a direct communication with his audience that most storytellers never achieve. The farm family is enthralled by his exploits. He generates a response, whether the gruff questioning of the father, the shy admiration of the daughter, or the hero worship of the little boy who, as Pauline Kael says, wants "to grow up to be just like Waldo."[2] The immediacy and stimulation are, however, present only in this performance. In the many other meetings between performer and audience that occur in the film the artistic efforts are increasingly stylized and the relationship between artist and audience becomes more distant.

The remainder of the film presents a gradual devolution from the pastoral ideal, showing us the ways in which the traditional verities have been changed in the modern world. In the second sequence, for example, Waldo's encounters with Axel and Mary Beth, we have actions similar to those in the farm sequence; however, the nature of that experience has significantly altered. The sequence begins when Waldo spots Axel trying to work the same type of crowd he relies on for a living and lands to meet the competition. Axel tries to bully Waldo into serving as his aide, but Waldo gains his revenge when he unbolts the wheels to Axel's plane. In terms of Hollywood entertainment the scene seems a typical extension of the opening sequence: light, played for laughs, harmless. Nevertheless, there are several developments which merit consideration.

First, the crowd is no longer receptive to the idea of flying for a thrill. They resisted Axel's blandishments, and Waldo earns his money by selling them excitement they can watch rather than excitement they participate in. The crowd mindlessly cheers Axel's plight, unaware of what is involved in attempting to land a plane in a lake.

There is also a different response to the performers. Whereas Waldo was invited to share dinner in the first sequence, this audience seems satisfied to take home some remembrance of the performers. For example, just as Waldo waves Axel off, a man steps up and takes his picture, intent on acquiring a fixed and reusable memento of the experience. Third, the interaction between the performer and the crowd is different. While Waldo has no contact with the crowd at the pond, he eventually meets up with Mary Beth and shares a meal with her. Dinner with the family has been transformed to a snack in a diner, and Waldo's story, which with the farmer's family seemed a part of the meal, his payment, is here a device for keeping Mary Beth's attention. She's thrilled by the excitement of the story, but hardly in the same way as the young boy or the farmer's daughter. Additionally, this story, which earlier served as proof of Waldo's heroic stature, here becomes proof of his meretricious nature. In this less archetypal world the old stories and formulas no longer apply and the rosy glow of the earlier scene is dissipated. Like the alternating images in the pretitle sequence, these similar but contrasting episodes show two views of heroism. The first is traditional; the second reveals a more complicated, less comprehensible world where traditional values have no currency and expectations are contradicted.

Waldo, however, sees this change in fortunes as a result of bad luck. "It should've been me," he mutters to himself as Mary Beth and Axel leave, indicating his belief that fate has deprived him of the opportunity to prove his worth. He lies not to make his way with Mary Beth but rather out of a need to share in the glory that was aviation in World War I.

This deflation of the hero, a complete reversal of our expectations, is so short and apparently atypical that most viewers pass it over as a puzzling lapse in the story. Nonetheless, it serves as a sign that the story cannot be interpreted as a traditional narrative. In accounting for this variation, we must step back from the character and evaluate the concept that Waldo sees as a form of personal salvation, an end which justifies some dubious means.

The narrative, however, moves back to the familiar saga of a struggle toward a goal. In the long central portion of the film, dealing with Waldo's adventures in the air circus, we see Waldo working to attain the fame and material success he believes concomitant with the performance of the heroic deed. In the first scene we are introduced to Kessler—at least to his exploits—and learn that he is indeed the best pilot in the world, the mountain Waldo must climb if he is to achieve his dream. Waldo plans to reach that summit, along with his best friend Ezra, by performing the outside loop, the last great unrealized stunt. Ezra will design the plane, Waldo will fly it, and they will both, in Waldo's words, become "very rich and very famous." To reach that celebrity status, however, Waldo needs money, and consequently he joins with Axel to develop a barnstorming act for Dillhoefer's circus.

This turn in the plot, the tribulation before the expected triumph, is standard Hollywood fare, the testing in which the hero shows himself worthy to try for the prize. There is Waldo's struggle to

*The Great Waldo Pepper (Robert Redford) during his barnstorming days (with Philip
Bruns at left as Dillhoefer).*
(Credit: Movie Star News)

develop an act, resulting first in the comic crash into the barn (which
introduces the Maudie segment) and second in the elation of wing
walking. Once the act is perfected Waldo must endure the circus's
continued ups and downs and the threat they present to the realization of his dreams. Waldo also pays a price in his personal life in his
quest to become the best. The sequence at Maudie's farm shows
Waldo sacrificing the rewards of the American life for a "higher" goal.
Maudie is the American dream woman; she is loyal to and supportive
of Waldo, self-reliant, loving, and beautiful. She is proof of his virility,
and his leaving, while somewhat undesirable, is nonetheless a recognizable step in our hero's progress.

Waldo shares another trait of the traditional hero and that is his
support of individualism. When confronted with the threat of bureaucratic control, of the systemization of flying, Waldo rebels. He
fights against the depersonalization of the one activity he knows to be
a test of the individual's mettle. "Are you going to license the clouds?
the rain?" he rhetorically asks, chafing at what seems an unjust
intrusion of small-mindedness, an almost insurmountable barrier of
regulations that threatens his quest.

Yet despite the presence of these familiar features there are elements in the story which derail the traditional narrative and shift our
attention to the subject of heroism. There is a superficiality to Waldo,
an uncharacteristic dissatisfaction with the self, that is covered by an
association with the trappings of heroism, and there is the questiona-
ble motivation of striving for riches and fame. Throughout the film
Waldo projects happiness into the image of the heroic flier and
attempts to invest himself with those characteristics. The incident at
the diner is the clearest indication of this tendency, but there are
other smaller incidents as well. For example, after the first air show
the camera cuts to a sign that reads "Lessons . . . Rides . . . Stunts
. . . The Best in the Area" and then pans to reveal Waldo's broken-
down plane in an empty field. The visual contrast between the
projected image of the self and the actual situation reveals Waldo's
myopia concerning his actual status. He willingly ignores anything,
such as his poverty, which threatens his quest or his image of himself.
When Waldo hears Mary Beth calling him, he throws down his rags,
dons scarf, cap, and goggles, and jogs out to meet her, the image of
boyish gallantry. It is, apparently, only in this guise that he feels
confident. Like Axel with his "Stunt King" sign, Dillhoefer with his
ever-changing circus sign, and Mary Beth with her "It Girl" banner,
Waldo advertises himself as someone worthy of note. Indeed, the
characters in the film seemed compelled to exaggerate their qualities,
as if a larger-than-life image is the only force that can lift them out of
the ordinary world. In post–World War I America it is the attaining of
the title, the acquiring of the rewards of heroism, that is as important
as living the ideas that once informed the notion of heroism. There is a
contradiction in the understanding of the concept, apparent to a
viewer, that hobbles the characters.

Another indication that Waldo is not a traditional hero is shown
through a comparison of his character with Axel's. Ordinarily the
protagonist's friends lack some essential element of character or
strength that prevents them from reaching the goal they seek; by
definition, only the hero possesses all the characteristics necessary to
achieve success. Here, however, Waldo does not benefit by comparison with those around him. Axel, for example, serves as Waldo's
doppelgänger, the moderate plebian self he could have become, and
surprisingly comes off well in the comparison with Waldo. Not only
do both men work the same profession and use the same line, but
they are dressed similarly and mirror each other's gestures (the
salutes) during their first meeting. They share the same background.
Waldo wished to be in the 14th Scouts and identifies himself with that

group; Axel was in the 14th Scouts. They have similar wartime experiences, are attracted to the same girl, and become a performing team. Axel's actions, then, can be seen as an implicit comment on Waldo's.

The most obvious contrast between the two men occurs in the scene following Mary Beth's fall. Her unexpected death shocks Axel into the realization that death is a part, perhaps the greater part, of the search for glory. He abjures the aggrandizement of self, calling the stunt flying "kid stuff," and retires from the air circus. Waldo, while he may regret Mary Beth's death, is more aroused by the threat of bureaucratic regulation, as it appears in the flaccid form of Newton Potts. He argues with Newt, having already forgotten the girl. While Axel finds a sober lesson in the tragedy, Waldo sees only a temporary pause in his march to glory. Another sharp contrast occurs in the Hollywood sequence. Axel hires on to do stunt work because he needs the money to establish a normal life; Waldo hires on out of a need to fly, jumping at the opportunity, seemingly lost, to prove himself.

There are also similarities among Waldo, Mary Beth, and Ezra, for all three are motivated by a need for success. In the latter two we see the nearsightedness and lack of understanding that can lead to fatal mistakes. Mary Beth is an extreme case. She is so infatuated with the idea of fame that she loses her grip on reality, becoming unable to distinguish between her dreamworld (that of Hollywood films) and her waking life. She wholeheartedly accepts the simple stereotypes and values of the Valentino film, and her infatuation with romance makes her easy prey for Waldo's line in the theater and his story. Later, she accepts Dillhoefer's offer to stardom, seeing the dangerous stunt as an easy route to unparalleled fame. The self-proclaimed " 'It Girl' of the Skies," naively thinking in terms of her movie magazines, makes a fatal error in judgment. Ezra makes a similar tragic mistake, overestimating his abilities and overextending himself in an attempt to win glory.

Waldo is pushed by a need for glory and afflicted by a similar blindness to the costs and dangers of his quest. He can give up Maudie, watch Mary Beth and Ezra die, and never question his goal, himself, or the significance of his actions. He learns nothing from experience, particularly if it does not match his preconceived notions of what life should be. His obstinance in pursuit of a goal becomes a proof of his limitations, not his virtue.

The most dramatic evidence of Waldo's nonheroic stature is his failure to rescue Mary Beth and Ezra. Convention demands a hero demonstrate his worthiness to receive our approbation, but *Waldo Pepper* surprisingly shows us someone incapable of effecting meaningful action. The sequence with Mary Beth is particularly striking because it is built in a conventional manner and there is no indication that we will see anything other than a rescue. Despite all his heroic exertions, however, Waldo cannot save the girl, and the audience is confronted with a failed figure. This reversal of expectations is not mitigated by a return to the traditional story line; instead we almost immediately witness Ezra's crash and gruesome death and Waldo's failure to save him.

Although these two deaths are extraneous to the traditional story (for they neither give the hero any needed insight nor help him advance his struggle in any perceivable way), they, in combination with the earlier reversals of the expected narrative, help crumble the traditional notion of the hero. Waldo seems more an inept dreamer than someone worth emulating, and consequently his ideals and motivations come under scrutiny. The honored concepts of heroism and success, so easily recognized in Waldo's actions and beliefs, are here given interpretations alien to those found in most American movies. His tenacious pursuit of heroism, both as a noble ideal and as a means to material success, blinds Waldo to the world around him, bringing unhappiness to himself and death to others. The results of his action pose, for both Waldo and the audience, a question about the nature of these guiding concepts.

In addition to developing the traditional plot and creating a different perspective on the genre subject, the middle portion of the film also shows the degeneration of popular art. Dillhoefer's air circus is a long way from Waldo's simply unadorned tale, but the two are nonetheless related. Each is an attempt to bring some part of the experience of flying before the public, though the goals, methods of presentation, and results are dissimilar. Dillhoefer's circus is a simple, stylized world far removed from the transcendent euphoria of Waldo's story. Dillhoefer's world is pure surface, offering titillation in return for money. The stunts are manufactured, and the danger never as imminent or threatening as it seems. With Waldo the presence of death is a real part of the world and one of the factors which makes it attractive.

Hustling, for Waldo and Axel, was born out of need or rivalry, a spur of the moment adventure. Dillhoefer has refined it to an art, and lives only to repeat the same sales pitch over and over. The crowds are different, too. Earlier, people had pressed around Waldo and Axel; now, they are formally set apart. The first audience, the farm family,

had only curiosity about Waldo and his life; the later crowds covet not
personal contact or information, but rather the most primitive forms
of stimulation. They evidence a morbid curiosity, heartily counting
during the "death spin" of Kessler and later gathering like vultures
around Ezra's crashed plane. If there is any interest beyond the
visceral, it is not in sharing or learning about flying, but rather in
duplicating the apparent benefits of a performer's life: celebrity status
and money. And, obviously, the appeal to the crowd is quite different. Waldo promised the crowd excitement, glossing over the danger
to Axel because he knew Axel could land in the pond. Dillhoefer's
whole sales pitch is danger. "I deal in sudden death," he tells Waldo.
"I don't want the crowd to think you're gonna die, I want them to
know you're gonna die." The result of these changes is that flying, the
phenomenon that motivates Waldo and gives him so much pleasure,
is lost. The crowd learns nothing of the glory, excitement, or pleasure
of flying, and the ideals that motivate Waldo are, at best, only vaguely
transmitted. Dillhoefer, and others like him, use their skills to make
money. For example, when Waldo first succeeds in wing walking, he
is alone on the wing, the sound of the motor gone, experiencing a
pleasure and exhilaration few can know. Yet we cut from that to
Dillhoefer barking out "the wing walking wonders of the world,"
cheapening what is beautiful without any concern for the loss.

By the time the air circus portion of the story ends, the primary
thematic and narrative developments are clear. Waldo the traditional
hero is mired in an increasingly desperate attempt to achieve his
dream of becoming the greatest flier in the world. There is also a
second narrative, paralleling the first, which, in its implicit negative
comments, questions the genre's assumptions. While Waldo proclaims that the world of heroic endeavor is still alive and a viable
avenue to success, we see a world in which heroic ideals have been
abandoned and in which heroic deeds are no longer possible. From
the risk and daring Waldo believes in to the safety and passivity
represented in Newton Potts and the faceless crowds, the world has
changed. Waldo, like such other Hill protagonists as Billy Pilgrim and
Butch and Sundance, ignores the overwhelming evidence that his
way of life is outmoded and clings instead to his romantic notions. The
question posed in this second narrative is not whether Waldo can
succeed in his quest, but rather whether he can understand his
dilemma in time to save himself.

For the viewer there is an additional dimension to the problem.
The contrast between Waldo's ideal world and the less attractive one

we encounter raises questions as to the worth, the true nature, the place of Waldo's traditional vision. Is heroic endeavor a combination of the noble and the material? Can it have economic value in the changed world? Where does it fit in to the new order?

Finally, we see popular art evolving into something lifeless, incapable of exploring or understanding the subjects that it treats. It remains to be seen whether there is an alternative to the shallow, manipulative tactics exemplified in Dillhoefer's circus.

In the Hollywood sequence these three strands come together and are resolved. The victory over Kessler is the expected ending, proof of Waldo's virtue and skill, and to the cynical or undiscerning viewer distressingly false or satisfyingly predictable.

The second narrative is resolved through Waldo's disappearance into the clouds, an unexpected twist which not only shows Waldo's growth to a knowledge of his position, but also indicates how we are to judge the traditional ideals. In the early part of the Hollywood sequence, Waldo remains an attractive figure, enduring the duplicity of the Hollywood stages and nourishing his dream of flying. Although his Hollywood existence remains a dead end, and his ideas are still fixed on the past, his world is turned around when he is hired to do stunt work on a film about the famous Kessler-Madden battle. He not only gets a chance to fly, but he also meets Kessler and at last takes the test that has meant so much to him.

The meeting with Kessler is a turning point, although not in the way Waldo expects. He is initially confused by Kessler's status and attitudes. To Waldo, Kessler is a hero, someone worth emulating, and thus he cannot understand why the German ace has made so little of his advantages. Instead of success, adulation, and happiness, Waldo finds that Kessler is anonymous, with an unhappy personal history, and is broke as well. Indeed, Kessler's story parallels his own. Kessler had known glory during the war, a transcendence of the quotidian world, and then a gradual but nonetheless permanent fall from that triumph. He has gone from the purity of flying to performing in air shows to doing stunt work in a Hollywood movie. Having seen firsthand the disparity between the heroic ideal and its value in the actual world, Kessler is not, like Waldo, surprised by the changes in and the superficiality of the Hollywood version of his story. But, like Waldo, he is forever held by the heroic moment of the famous dogfight. To Waldo's question of fear he answers that "no, everything was in order; the world made total sense." His answer parallels Waldo's version of the story at the farmer's table, where Waldo replied to a similar question with the words "everything was in order." The meeting, instead of showing that heroism is a valuable commodity, forces Waldo to evaluate the goals that have absorbed him. He is, in effect, asked what purpose his quest for perfection can serve.

Waldo's answer to that question remains vague until the dogfight with Kessler. Both men seem to realize that the mock battle is a unique opportunity, and they leave parachute and eventually the safety of playacting behind. Waldo's victory, which is seen by those on the ground as a triumph, is something different to the two pilots. For them, the outcome is less important than the experience of measuring themselves against each other, of knowing the harmony that can be found in the transcendent realm of testing against the ideal. After the victory Waldo pulls his plane alongside Kessler's and the two men exchange salutes. That gesture, which has been hollow throughout the film (witness Waldo and Axel's mock salutes to each other when they first meet and Waldo's final salute to Newt), again takes on its original significance: a signal of respect. Then Waldo glances at the ground and the surrounding sky, debating his course of action. He has reached an understanding of his position and knows he must choose between the ideal world where the heroic verities still have meaning or the modern world, which has completely disowned them. He drifts off into the clouds and to death (the final still photograph, suggesting Waldo has joined the ranks of heroes, has dates which indicate an early death). Such a resolution is rare in Hill's work for two reasons. First, the protagonist is given a chance to understand his dilemma, and second because the virtues of the heroic ideal are not viewed as false or debilitating, but rather as a concept that once had value and which, regretfully, has lost its meaning. It is a bittersweet view, a judgment not so much against characters who have been blinded by the ideal as against a society which has warped it.

The Hollywood sequence also allows Hill to conclude the developments concerning narrative and performance. At first, Hollywood seems the unpleasant culmination of all the negative tendencies apparent in the earlier performers in the film. From Waldo's benevolent manipulation of the crowd, the art of storytelling has evolved through Dillhoefer's calculated show, trading on death, to the fabricated world of Hollywood. In a familiar sequence, showing Waldo's work as a stunt double, we see the superficiality of Hollywood. The film industry is also disquietingly impersonal. When we first meet Werfel he is calmly watching the footage of a crash that injured a pilot, concerned primarily with the fact that the footage can be used twice.

Werfel is Dillhoefer refined: The barker's voice and carnival mentality are replaced by polished diction and professional showmanship. Werfel is also more skillful at entertaining and titillating his audience. Whereas Dillhoefer hawked his wares from town to town, Werfel uses the movies, the most successful form of mass communication, to help him sell. The audience, far removed from the action in Dillhoefer's circus, is now physically nonexistent, an apparently insatiable maw that feeds only on excitement. Accompanying the sophistication of technique is a diminution of understanding. Whereas Dillhoefer knew he was purveying death, Werfel has convinced himself that he is doing society a favor by turning out his treacle. When, for example, Waldo points out several factual errors between the Hollywood version and the real story, Werfel grandly replies that "anyone can provide facts; artists supply truth." The practitioners of popular culture, as exemplified by Werfel, have not only lost contact with the audience, but with themselves and with the material. Werfel's understanding of flying is far from the feelings we have heard Waldo describe and occasionally seen him experience.

The film medium, however, does not remain irretrievably false, for Waldo is able to use films to reach a better understanding of the concept of heroism. In his meetings with Kessler, Waldo begins to test his ideas against what Kessler has experienced, discovering that the notions presented in Werfel's picture are untrue, and that heroism's other attraction, the opportunity to test one's self against the highest standard, is more valuable. As Waldo loses his old ideas, his dream, so long unreachable, begins to materialize: Waldo is seen in the outfit of a young pilot and then as Madden, the hero of the legend. Waldo's break from the old notions comes when he rejects Werfel's script and goes off to fight Kessler. He uses the production elements of the film to catapult himself into what has been a dream, eclipsing time and physical limitations, and creates something that has true personal meaning. Unlike Mary Beth, who lost herself in the excitement of popular media, or the crowds, which only sought stimulation, Waldo gains something from the popular medium because he participates in it and refuses to be led by it.

While few people have the opportunity to use film's production effects, all have the chance to participate intellectually and spiritually, to test the film against their own experience and to learn, if possible, from their involvement. Waldo's actions implicitly argue for an alert, skeptic, independent, and imaginative viewer who can move beyond the passive acceptance of conventional wisdom. The portraits of Werfel and Dillhoefer also demonstrate that there must be a more concerned and honest treatment of the material by the artist. Werfel's film is "a lie," as Kessler says, because it is not interested in exploring a subject but rather in stimulating a response. These deceptive and trite notions must be left behind if popular art is to move past its status as sideshow attraction. While *Waldo Pepper* does not achieve the synthesis of entertainment and illumination it suggests is possible, it is notable—rare among American popular films—for suggesting film can go beyond tired formulas to something new.

6

Slapshot

IN *SLAPSHOT* George Roy Hill turns to the modern era and explores a subject seldom touched on in American film: sports and their effect, as a social institution, on the people who participate in them. Films about the various sports have long been a small, but regular part of Hollywood's output, but few movies have used sports as anything more than a backdrop to more traditional romances and melodramas (*Bang the Drum Slowly, Rocky, Angels in the Outfield, Somebody Up There Likes Me, Lou Gehrig Story*, the made-for-television *Brian's Song*). The standard themes are the importance of playing the game properly, the spiritual rewards of dedication, or the proving of one's self as an individual through competition. In these films sports serve as a standard of success, much as did the showdown in a Western film; the big game provides a convenient arena for the individual to test himself and prove his skills. Sports are also the great equalizer, the one part of our society free from the hobbling restraints of economic class, race, petty bureaucracy, or mundane life.

The primal appeal of sport has been channeled to the American public not by film, but by television, which, in the last two decades, has saturated the audience with every conceivable type of contest. In addition to presenting the contest, television and the print media have developed a particular way of looking at sports. In keeping with the sanitized vision of the world championed by television, and consonant with the owners' desire to appeal to a broad audience, the various sports media have propagated a gospel of sports as a healthy, clean, character-building, family-oriented activity. They have been so successful in their presentation, and have so clearly met a need,

91

Paul Newman with teammates in action in Slap Shot.
(Credit: Jerry Ohlinger)

that sports have become the great national avocation, and are seen as a pristine crucible in which the finest character virtues are brought to the fore.

Consciously or not, our society lionizes the star athletes, according them recognition, influence, and wisdom out of proportion to their accomplishments, and they in turn have used this popularity to achieve extraordinary financial rewards. It is not unusual then that the prospect of a life in or association with sports is obsessive for many. Additionally, professional sports franchises and amateur sports programs have become the center of social life in communities to the point that people identify with the teams, assuming for themselves the characteristics associated with the athletes. In communities which lack this token of identity, inordinate amounts of energy and money are spent trying to build up a professional, minor league, college, high school, or grade school program.

Inevitably, however, there are cracks in the flawless portrait. Despite the best effort of the sports establishment, the criticism of sport, particularly in books and magazine articles, has begun to flourish.[1] Authors point out the problems athletes have; talk about personality disorders, indifferent mercenaries, or widespread drinking or drug usage; excoriate sports for excessive violence or character-warping competitiveness; call the franchise, the city-state of sports, faltering, mismanaged, or unsuccessful; and worst of all suggest that the constituent elements of sports myth, the importance of winning and the inherent shaping of character, are false. Such departures from the ideal, while superficially threatening the reputation and popularity of sports, are often turned to the advantage of the prevailing ideology. Violence and intense competitiveness are transformed into "hard hitting," "aggressive," or "cleanly fought" play; franchises "struggle for respectability," or are in the "process of rebuilding"; and problem players become "troubled young men" whose difficulties coping with the world only make them more human. Through the magic of the word, the sports media perpetuate the old illusions while tailoring the new situations to a changing audience. The rare catastrophe or unrepentant player is relegated to the back pages and quickly forgotten; self-censorship by the media keeps the golden goose shining brightly.

Hill's film is one of the few commercially made movies to venture criticism of this social phenomenon. As usual, the results of Hill's analysis are presented ironically, and recognition of the criticism is dependent upon the audience's perception that the film does not fit into the classic test-resolution mode characteristic of most Hollywood and television sports epics. The characters in *Slapshot*, while apparently triumphing, are more accurately trapped in a no-win situation. They are typical Hill protagonists, blindly believing in transmitted social notions and at the same time demonstrating through their actions and statements the falsity of these ideas. Instead of giving them happiness, the pursuit of the ideals of sport keeps them in a perpetual state of adolescence that cannot be resolved by a change in scenery or a promotion. Hill suggests that the players, and the fans who support them, are duped because the noble ideals which inspire them do not adequately reflect human nature or the instincts of the social group to which they belong. Their pursuit of fame is shown as a waste of energy of such proportions that it calls into question the media-propagated assumptions about the sanctity of sports.

The scope and tone of Hill's enquiry is established in the opening shot. An American flag, draped over a scoreboard, fills the frame as the national anthem sounds tinnily through a second-rate loudspeaker. We are in middle-class America, a region where the spectrum of beliefs associated with sports is fervently accepted, where all the accoutrements of the myth have been emplaced, but where, inexplicably, the pieces refuse to come together in a coherent ensemble. Charlestown has a hockey team in the required gear, an arena, cheerleading sportscasters, but nothing in the way of the supposed benefits. The team loses consistently, the few fans are there to harass rather than cheer the players, the athletes endure such trials as the fashion show instead of enjoying the perquisites of stardom, and the town is on the verge of financial collapse. This is minor league sport, the obverse of the paradisical world of professional sport; it is sustained primarily by the faith of the players, who see the ordeal as a springboard to the pros, and the fans, who find in it an accessible source of dreams and entertainment. That this world, with all its failings, can still uphold the ideals of sport testifies to the strength of those conceptions and to the latitude of the conditions they sustain. The Chiefs in their incompetence and futility are more representative of sports than the professional teams they imitate, and they are a microcosm for the examination of the larger subject.

If the situation is different from the ideals of the adolescent sports legend, the players are equally distanced from the role models glorified in the media. They are crude, lewd, and permanently second string; they fritter away most of their time watching television. They are incapable of intelligent conversation and fixated on the female as a sex object. While it is impossible to classify them as heroes, they are excellent examples of the athlete as antihero, trashing confectionary sports values by exaggerating the primal elements of sex, violence, and freedom from responsibility. The appeal of such an image, similar to the appeal of the outlaw in country music, the trucker, or other renegades from society, is in the freedom these characters have from the drudgery of daily work, familial responsibility, and financial trouble. Films such as *Smokey and the Bandit*, *Animal House*, *Honeysuckle Rose*, and others of the good-old-boy ilk have struck paydirt by celebrating characters who have escaped bourgeois society and satisfied any number of daydreams. It is tempting, given the basic situation and characters, to see *Slapshot* as the sports version of this formula, a "National Lampoon Goes Skating." Hill, however, takes the simplistic situation and develops a comprehensive and complex treatment of the subject.

One key to the film is the variations Hill works on expected character types, for the athletes have two problems not associated with either the hero or antihero: they lack any insight into their situation and they have problems relating to women. Reggie Dunlop, the team's player-coach (Paul Newman, in his third film with Hill), is the prime example. His life seems a one-note symphony, a perpetual round of games, lounge bars, bus rides, seedy locker rooms, and the subdued thrill of competition. The highlight of the opening game, for example, is getting a drunken player to urinate in his pants. Whatever motivates Reggie to endure such a life is at first unclear, but its hold is powerful; Reggie has been in the game so long he has become sensitive to questions about his age. That such a life may be undesirable, that he is a failure at it, or that such a life-style can be threatened are questions which never occur to Reggie; he is so absorbed with his career that he must be hit squarely between the eyes before he notices his surroundings. For example, he is oblivious to the fact that he is beyond the age where National Hockey League stardom, or even employment, is plausible, and he conveniently ignores the evidence of his failure. When his ex-wife tells him he is a lousy coach, he talks of the bright future and how well things are going; when she indicates that they will not get back together, he smiles and perseveres in his wooing of her. For him such possibilities do not exist. When Ned Braden informs him that the factory will close and that the town faces a dreary economic future, Reggie dismisses it as a rumor. Braden's refutation stumps him for a moment, but he is incapable of worrying about the closing or believing that it will really affect him. He learns of the team's demise only when Braden reveals the general manager's job hunt, and Reggie, having never thought beyond the present, is as dull and imperceptive as the others. He retains a vague and unfounded hope that something will turn up.

While the other players, Mo, Johnny, Denis, Carlson, etc., are even more limited than Reggie, Ned Braden seems a pillar of intelligence. He is far more alert and sensitive to situations than Reggie, and is never fooled by Reggie's rah-rah pep talks or his Florida-sale plan. Yet despite his education, intelligence, and promise, Braden is nonetheless blind to selected parts of his world. He is convinced that he can somehow avoid the entombment in minor league hockey that Reggie and the others have fallen into, believing he is destined, apparently, for stardom. He also avoids acknowledging the fact that his marriage is a shambles and that his attitudes are a major cause of its demise. Lily Braden cannot stand Charlestown or the bleak future she sees ahead; she only asks that Ned take a job and that they get out of their second-class existence. She knows that Ned, unlike the others, has the skills, intelligence, and opportunities to do something else. However, Ned refuses to listen because he, like the others, is determined to prove himself through sports, no matter what the personal cost, and do something else later.

The unstated unifying trait among all the characters is their need to prove themselves through athletics. They do not want to go back to blue-collar jobs, or settle down, or build relationships with their wives because they share a belief in the old dream that success in athletics will resolve their personal problems and bring them recognition, material rewards, and spiritual satisfaction beyond that achieved by mere mortal men. Like Reggie, Ned and the rest are dreamers.

A second shared characteristic is the inability to communicate with women. For the players, women are necessary objects. The men need them as testimony to their virility and to provide emotional support, but they do not takes their wives' needs seriously. The precariousness of the athlete-woman relationship is developed most clearly in the Reggie-Francine, Ned-Lily, and Reggie-Lily subplots. Reggie continually campaigns to win Francine back; he calls her, chases after her in restaurants, goes out of his way to meet her, and is "crazy" about her. In one sense, she represents a great deal to him. However, despite the level of Reggie's effort, the campaign fails. Appropriately, Reggie often cannot make contact with his wife; his phone calls are interrupted, or he gets a wrong number, or he runs out of change; he just misses her at restaurants; and even his successful meetings are inconsequential. Reggie usually apologizes, complete with a glib story of why he has not called, asks her if she would like to get back together, and then stumbles for conversation. In short, Reggie has nothing to say to his wife that he has not said many times before, and her growth past his limited world leaves him confused. His need for Francine is not based on sex (he obviously can get that), or great passion (witness his apologies for not contacting her), but on the need to fill out one of the great requirements of the sports myth: a good athlete has a pretty wife sitting at home providing quiet support.

Ned Braden, as noted earlier, is also tormented by marriage problems. Ned not only will not accede to Lily's demands for a different life, but callously flaunts his infidelity and indifference. He does not mind if he is seen in public with other women or if his indiscretions are obvious; he does not attempt to curb Lily's drinking or alleviate her depression. In his world, complete, unthinking loyalty is Lily's only acceptable position. Proof of Ned's obstinate commitment to sports over his wife is his reaction to her defection to Reggie. His pride is stung, but he does not alter his plans: he is willing to give her up for a career in sports.

Reggie's relationship with Lily is more casual than Ned's. He seems, at first, to feel some need to seduce her and treats her much as he would a pickup. Once he wins her, he is equally insensitive to her problems and seems unaware that she is suffering. Part of his attention results from a need for sexual conquest, part from an attempt to goad Ned into playing his brand of hockey, and part from an attempt to make Francine jealous. Although the motivation is different, the situation is basically the same; Reggie regards Lily as an object to be used, a tool necessary to attain his goals.

In each case, the athlete has placed his career above the needs of the woman with whom he shares his life. Both have so unquestioningly accepted the rituals and beliefs associated with sports that their actions and perceptions are preordained. They evaluate each person or event in their lives in terms of how it fits into the established pattern of the archetypal athlete's life, so that they have unwittingly defined narrow limits to their intellectual and emotional growth.

For their part, the painted, coifed, and vacuous wives are perfect accomplices to the athletes' dreams. The women may talk of their loneliness and frustration, but they cannot conceive of an alternative to their dreary lives. Lily Braden rebels against her husband's obsession by resorting to drink and finally by leaving him for Reggie, but that maneuver is a mistake since Reggie is the model upon which Ned is based. Only Francine, with her good-natured insistence on her own life, escapes the no-win situation.

Although Hill unflatteringly presents the players as limited, failed, and out of touch with women, the players are far from capable of self-examination on such subjects. If their dealings with these problems serve as an example, they accept the consequences of their actions as part of the dues they must pay on the road to stardom. Hill's method of development, the gradual accumulation of detail, and his method of presentation, the subordination of the serious elements to the comic, mutes his criticism and avoids sermonizing. Nothing dramatic happens, there are no great changes, no sudden insights, no renewed commitments to ideas or people. Instead the character elements stand as relevant extenuating evidence that complements the central narrative tension in the film: the big question for the players, the one they perceive as the crucial test of character, is the decision to play "aggressive hockey," a euphemism for an extremely violent approach to the game. It is the differing views on violence, and the results those views produce, that raises issues about the basic nature of sport and its effect on athletes.

While few players or fans are concerned with the effect that sports, as an institution, have on the personality, all have or demonstrate an attitude toward the game. The expectations and beliefs revealed in the attitude are indicators of the real nature of sport and the social temper that fosters and condones it. Hill's film shows that violence in sport is organic, and that the appeal of the game is as much to the visceral as to the finer instincts. Far from being the test of self or the crystallization of civic bonhommie, as suggested by the sports media, sports is depicted as a controlled gladiatorial contest, a lightning rod for the audience's violent instincts. The fans, in turn, encourage and demand violent play before they supply the perquisites of adulation and support. The institution that has evolved hypocritically asserts for itself a simplicity and a distinction from the commerce of the world that it does not possess and provides few of the rewards it promises to its followers.

The divergent views on aggressive hockey are exemplified by Ned and Reggie. Ned upholds the traditional position, emphasizing ability rather than the use of violence to prove that one has the sterner stuff which separates the stars from the participants and merits the proffered rewards of sport. His happiest moments are early in the film, when he has a chance to demonstrate his skill, and are independent of the team's fate. The reasons for his consistent refusal to "goon it up" are not obvious, but they can be deduced from his other actions. He can only call Reggie's tactics garbage, only belittle the results, and only tear down the facade of aggressive hockey, as he does in his interview with Jim Carr, if he passionately believes in the opposite. What is at stake for him is self-image, and Reggie's violent tactics, by reducing the quality of the game, demean the value of the test by which he sets so much store.

In the first part of the film, Reggie would probably agree with Ned. The two men are comfortable with each other, an indication of similar disposition, and Reggie originally finds the Hansons distasteful because their methods are inconsistent with professionalism. Yet midway through the story Reggie undergoes a transformation that enables him to advocate aggressive hockey and work to make violence the basis of his sport. This change results from a meeting with Suzanne Hanrahan, an old flame, from which he unexpectedly gains more control of his life and a new perspective on hockey.

After a night of sex, Suzanne and Reggie catch up on each other's adventures. She confesses she has tried lesbianism because of the loneliness and frustration she felt as a hockey wife; moreover, she has left her husband and feels no guilt or remorse over her actions. Reggie is, naturally, vaguely supportive, even though such things are out of the realm of his experience. Suzanne, however, upon hearing of Reggie's problems, offers him something much better than sympathy; she gives him a solution to his dilemma. She tells him not to accept things as they are, but instead to "use your imagination" to make things better. That remark is an epiphany for Reggie, a realization that he can alter the seemingly fixed events that affect him. Although he indicates no understanding of the imagination, he is intrigued by the concept that one can orchestrate events, and takes to this new tool like a child discovering language. When, for example, he learns that Suzanne's husband is crazy with jealousy and shame over her choice, Reggie successfully implements a plan (his taunting of Hanrahan) that helps win the next game.

The difference in Reggie can be seen through a comparison of his old and new selves. Before the insight, Reggie shares the mental opacity and victimlike acceptance of the other players, their environment (long days at the coffee shop watching soap operas and television game shows), and their concerns (sex, making it in hockey). News of the team's demise receives the same treatment as the team's losing streak or the collapse of his marriage: genial indifference. After the meeting with Suzanne, he takes charge of his life, and his new sense of power is quickly extended beyond saps like Hanrahan. He steps back from his daily activities and begins manipulating events to achieve certain goals, smiling as he sees his newfound powers work.

Reggie creates a scenario, the Florida interest in the team, and begins massaging the press and his players to make that dream a reality. Like Henry Gondorff and Waldo Pepper, two other Hill protagonists, Reggie becomes something of an artist, fashioning a world to achieve specific ends. In his adapting to situations, in his conning of the players, in his working of the crowds, he exhibits a surprising ingenuity; however, his imagination eventually fails him and his creation slips past his control. Reggie's creative and intellectual powers wither, much as his physical skills deteriorate with age, because his vision is dominated by the conventional perception of athletics as a heaven on earth. He finds one new way to reach his goal of stardom, and invests all his energies into the single activity of working the crowd; yet, because he has no perspective on himself or the larger social context, he can only create variations on his single insight concerning the crowd's needs. The limitations on this method are obvious. Instead of seeing that there is something wrong with the game or the crowd's ugliness, Reggie is forced to conjure up more and more violent scenarios (the bounty on Dr. Hook, for example) until the whole plan eventually collapses into the lunacy of the final game. Reggie, like the other Hill characters, becomes an example of negative imagination, of the way not to create.

At the same time that Reggie acquires the vision that enables him to use violence as a means to an end, he also discovers the perfect instruments to inject violence into the game: the Hansons. Whereas Reggie and Ned define the two different points of view on violence in sports, the Hansons are a vision of what would result if those two points of view were joined. From their first appearance—we see them mauling a soft drink machine which has failed to deliver a soda—the contradictory attributes of innocence and crude violence are simultaneously apparent. On the one hand they are models of athletic virtue, faithful adherents to the creed that Ned stands by. They prefer soft drinks and ice cream to beer, spend their time playing with toys rather than chasing women, have a healthy disdain for the obsequious members of the press, and are quintessential team players, mindlessly and enthusiastically echoing Reggie's every coaching cliché. If, like the other players, they recognize the triteness of Reggie's exhortations, they mask it with hearty cheering. Simultaneously, the brothers are the incarnation of mindless violence, nonpareil exponents of the new style Reggie urges his players to adopt. They are foul-mouthed goons who not only excel at their tasks but revel in the havoc they create. This violent tendency is also carried over into civilian life as well, as can be seen in their encounter

Paul Newman as Reggie Dunlop encourages aggressive hockey while Michael Ont-kean (Ned Braden) looks on.
(Courtesy: Museum of Modern Art/Film Stills Archive)

with a hapless hotel clerk. In combination, the two halves of their personality form a *reducio ad absurdum* of all the personality traits demanded by fans, coaches, and the media. They are a comic balance to the more serious conflict between Reggie and Ned, and, moreover, at the same time complement that struggle. They are exaggerated enough that the targets of the satire are clear, but realistic enough (there is a little of the Hansons in every jock) that the film does not disintegrate into silliness. The issue of violence remains viable until the conclusion of the film.

When the Hansons are unleashed they set in motion a sequence of events which shows the magnitude and the extent of violence in sports. In their first appearance, they transform the game. The early action scenes were confusing; the result of the efforts, a goal, arrived at haphazardly; and the players seemed more intent on their little joke with the drunken opponent than they did with the score. The fans booed with good reason. The Hansons are photographed in a different manner. Instead of an overview or an attempt to show continuity, Hill has a series of active, self-contained scenes, usually shot at medium distance, that give an invigorating sense of speed and excitement. The Hansons are shot as individual personalities, the focus of our attention, and their actions are readily comprehensible. Everyone can appreciate their slapstick stunts. In comparison with the other, going-through-the-motions players, the Hansons are whirling dervishes, and their actions shock teammates and spectators alike as they make a shambles of the traditional game. They reveal a potential for violence that few onlookers realized existed and, as they win, make that violence exciting and, more importantly, appealing. Reggie is delighted with the results of his plan, and the idea of aggressive hockey becomes valid and attractive.

The other players are somewhat reluctant to imitate that style, but eventually they dutifully follow the Hansons' lead. In so doing, they unexpectedly transform themselves into winners. Denis, the incompetent goalie, becomes a tiger on defense, and adopts a mask that objectifies this new image of himself. The others carry themselves with a new swagger as they find themselves objects of adulation. The most obvious change is in Dave Carlson. At first, he is the impressionable rookie, the naive kid learning the game; however, under Reggie's tutelage, he becomes not just another hockey player, but Killer Carlson, a terror of the ice whose violent play is characterized by childlike fervor. He starts wearing a Dracula cape and listening to self-help records to psyche himself into the appropriate berserker state necessary for the new game.

These changes in personality are not only a source of humor, but also show that violence is an inherent part of the contest, not something imposed by Reggie. This is seen, again, most clearly in Dave Carlson's metamorphosis. Reggie begins working on Dave by using an old ploy, feigning weakness from age and abuse from the opposition. In his pitiable state he asks Dave's assistance and support. Later, in the midst of a brawl, Dave instinctively goes to Reggie's rescue and joins the ranks of the wild-eyed brawlers. He loves it, and converts wholeheartedly to the new style. The violence is in his nature, not an alien idea, and unfettered it mushrooms out and quickly overcomes his personality. The team, which once eschewed the tactics of legendary goons like Oggie Oglethorpe, adopts that style when they find it leads to winning.

As Reggie soon discovers, the fascination with violence catches up with more than just his players. After one victory Reggie finds the bus driver smashing holes in the bus to "make it look mean." A new set of fans appears, even on road trips; they are loud and boisterous, share the same rules-be-damned attitude (for example, the community mooning for the old-time hockey fans), and the women are beautiful and buxom enough to satisfy every player's fantasies. They like violence, and support the team because they get it. Judging by the increasing size of the crowds, they are also more numerous than the fans who enjoy the traditional version of the game. Together, players and fans discover that violence in sports, contrary to conventional wisdom, can be both rewarding and fun.

Reggie, however, gradually becomes dismayed at the increasing success of his scenario. He had intended only to stir up the players to create enough interest in the team that someone would save the franchise. When people enthusiastically embrace his idea, he is both disgusted and perplexed. He never, any more than Ned, consciously thought of the Hansons' style of play as the essence of hockey, as his many years of service in the minor leagues testify. As Ned, however, underestimates the appeal of violent sports, Reggie underestimates the pervasiveness of violence in all parts of our society. Hockey is not a separate phenomenon, but a part and reflection of the larger human context. Aggressive hockey sells because people want to buy it.

Nowhere is the infatuation with and the tacit condonement of violence more apparent than with the two sports media figures, newspaperman Dickie Dunn and broadcaster Jim Carr. Dickie impresses by his obtuseness; a perpetual hanger on, he turns each Chief performance, if we can judge by Reggie's comments, into poetry, a remarkable feat considering some of the Hansons' tactics. Dickie can perform such alchemy with sincerity because he is insensitive to all but the romantic aspects of the game. In the establishing shot for the one scene at Dickie's home, Hill shows two children watching a violent film on television and fighting over it. Dickie blocks out the noise, telling the children to settle it between themselves, and retreats into the safe subject of sports. He ignores his environment, unconsciously perpetuating it, because he is so easily satisfied by any spectacle which alleviates his humdrum existence. Violence, in sport or at home, is filtered out or turned into something attractive because that is easier than focusing the mind on difficult issues.

If Dickie is a great passive bulk, witlessly condoning violence, Jim Carr is the active promoter, the type who identifies winning hockey with good hockey. In the early scenes he is a perfect parody of the television sports reporter, asking mindless questions, converting every answer into a sports cliché, and cheerfully plowing on, no matter what the attitude of his respondent. His boyish joy at the winless Chiefs becomes near orgasmic ecstasy when they march toward the playoffs, and in the best home announcer tradition he begins to characterize the Chiefs' every action in a positive light. Violent, goon-squad hockey becomes aggressive hockey that is a model of sportsmanship, a pattern for youngsters to emulate, and a source of civic pride.

The hypocrisy of this view is exposed in his encounter with Ned Braden. Disgusted by the new style of hockey, Ned stalks to the broadcast booth during a game and gives vent to his anger. Carr, who at first maintains the pointless chatter and the play-dumb persona, becomes incensed when Ned violates the basic announcer-athlete rule against creating controversy. Ned's iconoclastic talk about sexual problems at home and attitude problems with the game is shocking, and Carr becomes as violent in his defense of civic virtues as Ned is determined to expose them. It boils down, at least for Carr, as to who is more of a man, for in Carr's simplistic view being a winner or being associated with one equals being a man. Whatever contributes to that ego-satisfying perception is acceptable and necessary for Carr and those who share those ideas.

The crowd, the mass served by Dunn and Carr, also exhibits an infatuation with violence. The sparse, indifferent group that booed the losing team's games are replaced by massive crowds that lustily cheer and imitate the violence on the ice. There is the key throwing incident at the away game, a fight among the crowd before the championship game, and snarling dogs used for crowd control. As Jim Carr and Reggie intuitively know, these people want violence in their entertainment, and Reggie runs ragged in order to meet the demand.

The madness initiated by the Hansons spreads to epidemic proportions. The insatiable demand for violence causes an escalation of the goon-squad tactics and other teams respond by bringing in players more violent than the Hansons. Violence is no longer a means to an end, it is now the game, and the only competition is at the most primitive physical level. The fervor sweeps up all but Reggie and Ned, for they alone stand back, saddened that sport, the pristine dream they both cherish, has disappeared beneath the endless combat.

The situation developed by Hill and screenwriter Nancy Dowd, while comically exaggerated, reflects the dilemma sports such as football and hockey find themselves in. The injection of more action to liven up the game diminishes the quality of the product, so much so that sport is replaced by entertainment. Moreover, the social value placed upon success in sports puts the athletes in an unpleasant bind. Faced with a need to prove themselves, and having only success as a standard of achievement, they abandon old ideals for a method, violence, that can guarantee their desired rewards. They, too, are cheapened in the process, for they become spiritually enervated, narcissistic, and self-deluded; the athlete as model of civic virtue disappears.

Hill not only shows the travesty of modern spectator sports, but suggests the farce continues because of our culture's infinite capacity for self-delusion. The unwavering belief in the sports myth, shared by athletes and spectators alike, serves as a modifying lens which depicts all actions as positive and responsible. As long as the game provides a stimulus to the fans' interest, and a winning team is the surest appeal, unsportsmanlike conduct will be encouraged and supported; it may be described in fine prose or pictured as an achievement, but nothing can change the fact that the game harms the players and is but sop for the fans. Hill's denouement shows the hopelessness of the players' situation. By the film's end the major characters are seen as failures trapped by the social institution into dead-end lives, their idealistic goals replaced by petty, foolish actions that stand out more forcefully than the victory the film supposedly celebrates.

Reggie, who has been the instigator of the events, eventually succumbs to the plot he has set in motion. Initially it appears he has kept sight of his goal, keeping the team alive until someone expresses interest. He is appalled at the success of his machinations, and it appears that only desperation has driven him to this point. But, after the encounter with Anita McCambridge, the owner of the team, it is difficult to accept Reggie as one truly aligned with the ideals of sport. Her decision to let the Chiefs expire makes Reggie angry, and it is then, only *after* he is certain there is no future with the Chiefs, that he decides to return to the principles of old-time hockey. The sequence of events demonstrates Reggie's insincerity; he has chased dreams for so long that he has compromised away all the honorable character traits he may once have had. Later, in his appeal to Ned to return to the game, this point is again made clear. Reggie catches himself lapsing into clichés to manipulate Braden and must struggle to get out an honest statement. Trapped by his need to fulfill an image, Reggie has become a shell without substance. His speech to the players about old-time hockey is an attempt to recapture his past, but that is jettisoned the moment he learns there are NHL scouts in attendance at the championship contest. In his final encounter with Francine there is perhaps a moment of doubt about his life, but he remains essentially unchanged: still lying to her about his feelings and to himself about his future.

Lily Braden is the big loser. Although she works up the courage to leave Ned, it is only the last gasp of a drowning woman. She meekly submits to Reggie's direction, and he, wanting not a liberated woman but a carbon copy of the standard hockey wife, takes her to Francine for refurbishment. Sensitive to Lily's plight, Francine gives her some feminine reassurance: with a little makeup and a new hairdo, Lily could "look just like Cher." Lily's appearance at the championship game is the ultimate capitulation. She is now just another cheery, bubble-headed wife, squirming at the excitement of the game, smiling and waving at her husband. At the film's end she is riding happily beside him, caught up again in the magic of sports.

Ned remains confirmed in his pursuit of stardom, and is given a second chance at it when Lily returns to him. Her appearance at the championship game in her new persona is the boost he needs to counterattack the idea of aggressive hockey. With Lily in her proper role as ornament and support, Ned demonstrates a little imagination of his own. He subverts aggressive hockey by taking an element of it, sexuality, that has been repressed, and exaggerates it. He leaps upon the ice and to the accompaniment of the band—and the delight of the crowd—strips down to his jock. The incident so disrupts the violent hockey game that the Chiefs end up winners by forfeit when the other team quits in disgust at Ned's perverse act. In making the hidden public, and in having it accepted by the crowd, Ned explodes the assumption that aggressiveness is the sole basis of the sport's popularity. He intends only to trash the farce of the championship game, just as Reggie and the others have ruined his old-fashioned ideals, but he inadvertently reveals that sex is a second wellspring of the sport's popularity.

Although this revelation appears sudden, in actuality Hill has carefully laid the groundwork for it. Throughout the film Hill shows that the players have limited ideas about sex and emphasizes their belief that there is a connection between success in sports and sexual prowess. The athlete as stud is a major source of humor in the film. There is Mo's unending series of lewd comments about "snatch," the brief scene with the ice show chorine who has slept with Oglethorpe, the egregiously pneumatic twins that chase after Billy (the narcissistic player), the pharmacy worker who becomes friendly with Denis, Johnny's exposure at the fashion show, and Reggie's attempts to bed Lily. While heterosexual sex is a straightforward matter for the players, anything diverging from that standard confuses them. For example, Braden's marital problems with Lily are inexplicable to them. Lily is an attractive woman and Ned's not sleeping with her

leads them to question his masculinity. But that questioning is rejected because, as Denis says, he cannot be a homosexual: "he has a
cock as big as a horse." This same concern with masculinity and fear of
homosexuality surfaces again with Hanrahan, who is manipulable
because he believes his wife's sexual choice reflects on his sexual
prowess. The other players share this view, for one of the Chiefs
wonders if Suzanne's lesbianism means that Hanrahan is queer.
Finally, when Reggie learns that his plan has failed, he abuses Anita
McCambridge with the most vile aspersion that he can think of: her
son (who is not being exposed to violent sports) will grow up to be a
homosexual. Although the players never consider the fact, the issue
of sexual identity is a major part of their lives, and success in sports is
seen as some sort of proof that one is a real male. Ned's striptease
focuses the sublimated concern with sex on a tangible act, much as
the Hansons' tactics made the lure of violence overt, and establishes
the importance of sex to sport. Whether it be the athlete as sexual
object for the female fan, or the athlete as sexual alter ego for the male
fan, sex helps make sports go.

Neither players nor fans reflect on the relationship between sex
and sports; as with violent play, it is viewed as a form of entertainment, a novelty which purists of the old school (such as Dr. Hook) find
unacceptable. There is another similarity to the response to violence
in that all is accepted and condoned as long as it leads to winning. Jim
Carr's frenzied denunciation of Ned turns to praise when Ned's strip
inadvertently leads to a Chief victory, and even Ned, who was
disgusted with the game, succumbs to the thrill of winning.

As the film ends, no one has learned from his or her experiences;
the characters are committed to the same life with, if possible, more
dedication. Hill's ironic film prevents such an easy acceptance for the
viewer. While the outline of the story is familiar, the case for sports is
exaggerated to the point that it falls apart. The transformation of the
Chiefs is not inspiring, nor even a modern reversal of the old ideals;
rather, the absurdity of it shows how hollow and false the accepted
sports conventions are. It is impossible, having seen the Hansons and
the crowd's reaction to them, having seen the strained relationships
between the men and women, and having seen the limitations of the
life-style, to believe naively in the old ideology. Instead of a spiritual
ethos, sports is shown to have its roots in the basic physical urges of
man: sex and violence. The games men play are substitutions for
cruder contests, a sublimation of these urges for both the participants
and spectators that has been shaped by social forces into an institution

that supposedly provides the most romantic and ideal virtues. Hill's film asks the viewer to reexamine the ritualized and sanctified institution by showing the personal price paid by the true believers. As the film ends, we are back at the starting point: a high school band is playing "Yankee Doodle Dandy" as an old time parade celebrates the athletes' accomplishments. Our belief, however, can no longer be as steadfast or as simple.

7

A Little Romance

A LITTLE ROMANCE (1979) marks another departure for Hill. It is his first film since *Hawaii* in which the characters are not viewed ironically, and it is his first romantic story since *Period of Adjustment*. In some ways it harks back to *The World of Henry Orient* in its depiction of bright adolescents learning the realities of adult life. For example, the female protagonists in the two films have similar home lives and problems. Val Boyd of *Henry Orient* has a business-oriented father, basically good, who has neglected his duties toward his child, while Val's promiscuous, suspicious, and selfish mother is the major source of conflict. Lauren King, the teenage heroine of *A Little Romance*, has a decent, though preoccupied stepfather, and an interfering, suspicious mother who makes her home life difficult. Each finds an escape from these problems in romance, although Val's is a fantasy. The two films differ, however, in their general tenor. *Henry Orient* shows the deflation of Val's romantic dreams and her salvation through her father's renewed commitment to family values; it is a film about learning which things in life have worth. In *A Little Romance* the teenage lovers have moved past adolescent fantasies; they have found a valuable kind of love which they struggle to keep pure from an adult world where self-indulgence has replaced true feeling. With a little help from an old con man (Laurence Olivier), they overcome the physical and emotional obstacles that threaten their budding relationship and break free of the culturally instilled perceptions about romance so blindly adhered to by the adults in the film. Despite the age of the protagonists, the story is a study of romantic love.

A Little Romance also continues Hill's exploration of film as a narrative art. Once again the subject matter concerns fiction making, and the story becomes a reflexive commentary on the narrative

109

process. The teenagers, at times, become artist figures who, unlike other such figures in Hill's films (the con men in *The Sting*, Reggie Dunlop, Waldo Pepper), serve as an alternative to contemporary modes of artistic creation rather than as negative examples of the creative process. Their adventure shows that, contrary to traditional assumptions, narrative works best when both artist and audience are conscious of the purposes and methods involved in the creation of a narrative, and when the audience imaginatively enters into and tests the values inherent in a fiction against their own beliefs and perceptions. The independence they declare from the established ways of creating and understanding a story becomes the key to a new narrative method.

On the surface, the film is decidedly romantic in tone, from the soft-focus photography and the appropriately gentle music (Vivaldi's Concerto in D) to the simple story line and the unabashedly sentimental conclusion. We follow two gifted adolescents as they strive to realize a romantic dream and reaffirm the eternal power of love.[1] Yet the story of their struggle and triumph is more than one of plot complication and happy resolution, for through the seemingly slight and engaging love story Hill explores several complex subjects. In addition to parents and police, the teenagers must also deal with sexuality and its place in their relationship and the problem of making that relationship endure and grow. Since society provides no set answers to these problems, their attempts to resolve them become in effect an examination of these subjects, much as the Hollywood romances of the 1930s and 1940s defined the proper attitudes and stances concerning love.

In their search for happiness the lovers first turn for guidance to the wisdom of the cultural past (romantic legends) and present (film), taking their cue for action from the attitudes implicit in these chosen mediums. When problems arise, the youngsters act according to established formulas in an attempt to resolve them; however, on at least two occasions (the visit to the porno house and the escape from Verona), they find that conventional wisdom fails them. In order to save their relationship, they must instead rely on their own imaginative and intellectual powers. Thus, in place of the tried-and-true precepts handed down by adults, they create a romantic legend to serve them as a guide. While this may seem an ordinary response, it is made unusual not only by the strength they derive from it but also by their self-consciousness that the legend is just a story they have agreed to believe in. Theirs turns out to be a different kind of romance, and the contrast between it and the expected conventional narrative focuses our attention on the cultural concepts which tacitly shape relationships between people. Rather than affirm old formulas, the solution to the teenagers' problem, as uncommon as the romance is traditional, opens up a familiar subject to investigation.

The film begins in a conventional manner. Our two teenage protagonists are worlds apart economically and socially, and the first part of the story details their discovery of a common ground and a growing affection for one another. Daniel is a self-reliant youth; he does the shopping and cooking, is a whiz at playing horses, and is intellectual light years ahead of his taxi-driving father. Yet that independence is part bluff, since Daniel suffers typical teenage anxieties about growing up. With a nonentity for a father, Daniel has become a dreamer who escapes from his everyday world through the movies. The first four shots of the film are clips from Daniel's favorite flicks which, not surprisingly, celebrate such male icons as Paul Newman, Robert Redford, John Wayne, Humphrey Bogart, and Burt Reynolds. Daniel so identifies with his idols that he adopts their gestures and expressions (for example, Burt Reynolds' "Bingo" and the finger pointed like a gun).

He also tends to view his life in terms of movies and falls back on film for reference and guidance. He introduces himself to Lauren, for example, as Bogey, making an allusion to the Bogart-Bacall marriage; qualifies a remark on Lauren's political beliefs with the phrase, "I've seen it in films"; toasts Lauren at her birthday party with Bogart's line, "Here's looking at you, kid"; talks knowingly of the Italian border guards and barbed wire they can expect on the trip to Venice and documents his case with his favorite proof: "I've seen it in films"; and he gives Lauren one of his most prized possessions, the supposedly autographed photo of Robert Redford. For him, films eclipse other forms of narrative. He knows some poetry, but does not value it as highly as film, and Julius's storytelling leaves him cold. Such an allegiance to and reliance on films is not unusual, but it suggests that Daniel is still at an unformed state where he has yet to learn to view the world with his own eyes.[2]

Lauren King is a bright, pretty, privileged teenager, but she, too, is not without problems. A bookish loner, she's uninterested in the world of films, to which she has some access, possibly because her mother is so obviously infatuated with the pompous director, George DiMarco. School is a bore, for she does not share the usual mindless concerns of adolescent girls, like her friend Natalie. Home is not a refuge, either; she is distanced from her mother, and her well-intentioned stepfather is unable to help her or relieve her disappointment. She also retreats into fantasies, but of a gentler nature, as indicated by her high regard for the poetry of Elizabeth Barret Browning and Julius's story of life with Emmaline.

When the two meet they discover a common ground: their intelligence, their disregard for fops like DiMarco and his hangers on, and their sense of isolation from home and their fellow teenagers. They can talk of these problems, and that establishes a bond between them; moreover, because they are distinct from their peers, cut off from the stock responses of someone like Natalie or Londet, they occasionally think about their problems and ways to resolve them. Their attraction grows, and the biggest stumbling block, at least on the surface, seems to be finding ways to meet each other and enjoy each other's company.

However, as their relationship develops, another, unarticulated aspect of it emerges and begins to cause them some difficulties. The question of sex, of whether or not to have it and how to regard it, assumes a larger importance for the two even though they seem unaware of its force. Having met, they, and most of the other characters in the film, subconsciously debate the question; the adolescents try to find some way to resolve it without embarrassing themselves, while the adults read their own romantic or lewd intentions into the relationship and act accordingly.

Sexual urges are typical of adolescence, as is confusion about sex, and Daniel and Lauren, despite their intelligence, modesty, and consideration for each other, have some problems approaching the subject. They are hindered, on the one hand, by peer pressure (in the form of the minor characters, Natalie and Londet), and on the other hand with the conflicting, confusing signals sent from the adult community.

Part of that confusion results because the adults, who serve as role models for the teenagers, have a dual perspective on sex. At times there seems to be a constant drive for it: witness Lauren's mother and her chase after DiMarco, the porno house, or the adult film the teenagers are not allowed to see. This concern also manifests itself in their actions (the flirting at the party, particularly Kay and DiMarco nibbling hor d'oeuvres) and their talk (DiMarco's lewd suggestions about Lauren; Broderick Crawford's stated desire to "get laid"). Yet this urge is also seen as something corruptible and dirty. There are repeated attempts to control sex, or awareness of it, apparently on the theory that it is unhealthy for the young.

This repressive aspect is most apparent in Lauren's mother, who, reading her own intentions into Lauren's actions, sees her daughter as a potential whore and her harmless birthday party as an orgy. The very suggestion of physical contact between the adolescents traumatizes her and, despite a lack of evidence, she attempts to separate Lauren and Daniel. However, there are also other, less direct attempts to control the teenagers. Daniel tries to take Lauren to see a film with Catherine Deneuve, but is denied admission because there is a brief nude scene. On their first date, Daniel is reluctant to kiss Lauren, not only out of shyness, but partly because a formidable matron is disapprovingly glowering at him. The guardians of middle-class morality discourage even the tentative stirrings of physical awareness. Perhaps the best example of this dual perspective on sex is found in Natalie, the brainless friend who faithfully mirrors the attitudes of the adult world. Natalie constantly talks and wonders about sex, quizzes Lauren with irrepressible eagerness, and yet is shocked when Lauren suggests that she and Daniel have "done it." So strong is Natalie's disapproval that Lauren must confess her joke, at which point Natalie once again reverts to her leering, inquisitive ways. It is as if direct public acknowledgment of the sexual act is sinful, and only innuendo or suggestion, some form of linguistic distancing, is an acceptable form of discourse. This hypocritical stance finds its adult expression in Kay King, who, despite her obvious sexual flirtation with DiMarco, is discomfited by Broderick Crawford's straightforward expression of lust.

Dealing with this contradictory attitude is difficult enough, but Lauren and Daniel also have their own problems. Daniel, who shapes so much of his life in terms of film, views sexuality as a necessary part of being masculine. In his favorite films, the competency of the male characters extends to the realm of sex, and these heroes never have problems finding it or difficulties dealing with it. Daniel must not only try to live up to that image (note his defensiveness whenever he does not succeed in an endeavor as well as he expects to), but he also must compete with the example of his friend Londet, who seems vastly experienced concerning women. Under these subtle pressures, Daniel seems compelled to bring sex into the relationship with Lauren. After they are refused entry into the Deneuve film, Daniel drags Lauren to the porno house, as if to prove that he is mature enough to handle sex.

Lauren is more reticent about sex, but it is nonetheless a concern for her as well. The two other major female characters in the film (her mother and Natalie) are both concerned with sex and assume that Lauren is ready for or already having a physical relationship with Daniel. They cannot help but remind Lauren of the subject, whether it be the example of the mother's affairs and marriages or Natalie's talk about boys, babies, and filling out. Sex also surfaces intermittently in acceptable formats, such as the nude statues at the Louvre which absorb the girls' attention.

In response, Lauren, like Daniel, pretends to a sophistication about sex (her joke with Natalie, for example), and to prove her maturity she follows Daniel into the porno house. But the film shocks her, and her unexpected flight leads to an unexpected resolution of the issue. The teenagers discover, after Daniel's apology, that there is a difference between love and sex, and decide to build their relationship upon their mutual interests and feelings for each other. Despite the meddling interests of friends and parents, Daniel and Lauren overcome this first test to their relationship; in opposition to the adult world, in which sex seems a spiritless pursuit of physical pleasure, they opt for a chaste, spiritual relationship.

At the same time that the lovers' story moves forward, Hill develops a theme revolving around the place and purpose of narrative art in our culture. A review of the action shows that there are various types of narrative present in the film, from carefully structured artifices, such as the film-within-the-film, to the casual white lies people use in everyday life. On the large scale of narrative there is film. Not only is there DiMarco's tawdry creation, but there is the porno film, and the allusions to successful motion pictures with broad popular appeal (*Butch Cassidy, True Grit*). There are also references to books; the Heidegger Lauren and Daniel read, the Nancy Drew mysteries that fascinate Natalie, and the poetry of Elizabeth Barrett Browning. These narratives, external to the characters, exert varying degrees of influence on them, from the all consuming interest of Daniel to the narrow interest of Lauren, and affect how they perceive the world. In some cases, such as Daniel's, the connection is clear; in others, such as Lauren's, the sources of the ideas are less obvious; and in still others, the adults, the sources are lost and only habits remain.

In addition to the multiplicity of types and differing degrees of influence from external sources of narrative, the characters in the film create their own fictions for personal use. Daniel, for example, in response to Lauren's admission that she has lied about reading the Heidegger, replies that he "lies all the time; you have to." He also imposes his film-shaped thoughts on his relationships and situations, attempting to correlate his physical experience with his cinematic experience. As Julius says, Daniel is always imitating Robert Redford.

DiMarco can be seen as structuring personal statements, albeit banal ones, on a grand scale. Kay King invents white lies to foster her relationship with DiMarco, though her stories share something of her phoniness. Finally, Julius, the con man played by Laurence Olivier, lives entirely on stories, creating a persona, complete with past, to fit a particular occasion and listener. His fictions are more successful than most, entertaining Lauren and inspiring her where others have failed.

While types of narrative play an essential role in the lives of the characters, there is no clear best type which benefits the individual. None of the narratives, public or personal, seem to work very well. External narratives affect, but seem beyond the control of the characters; personal narratives are either put to selfish ends (Kay King's lies) or else serve as a crutch for an individual's problems (Daniel's uncertainty about the world; Julius's lack of a presentable character). In the world of the film, the act of narrative seems unlearnable, a nebulous activity beyond discipline.

Yet the characters and events of the first half of the film at least show how *not* to fashion a story, and in so doing imply some of the qualities that would be a part of a useful and successful narrative. On the level of external narrative, DiMarco stands as an example of what has gone wrong with filmmaking. He has divorced himself from his material, recognizing neither the subtleties of the artistic process nor the purposes which the work can serve. He thus imposes a grand meaning upon his actions that is inappropriate to them and makes a fool of himself. In the making of his movie, apparently a cheap thriller, he asks the starlet to display a depth of emotion that is unnecessary, demanding an authenticity that cannot add to the film. He is unalert concerning the details of filmmaking (his confusion over the appearance of a door in the shot) and insensitive to people and situations (his tantrum over the mirror, his statement to the French about shooting in Spain). The pretension of his approach contrasts sharply with Broderick Crawford's straightforward concern for getting the job done in the easiest manner possible. Away from the set, when speaking of his film, DiMarco exhibits the same laughable pretension. When a patroness of the arts lavishes him with incoherent praise, he witlessly accepts it as his due. DiMarco, it appears, embraces fads in filmmaking, such as the worship of the director, as readily as he embraces fashion fads (his scout uniform), with equally disastrous results.

As DiMarco serves as an example of how not to make films, Daniel is a good model of how not to watch them. As noted earlier, the values and ideas inherent in certain popular films have replaced his own sense of judgment, and he views his life in terms of the films he sees. While DiMarco has little sense of the value of films, Daniel has absorbed and imputes to them a value most narratives cannot possess. For example, his fantasy life includes some of Broderick Crawford's work, and he is surprised to find that Crawford does not cherish it, or even remember it, as enthusiastically as he does. (However, this mild shock does not faze Daniel since he is glowing in Crawford's praise for his right hand.)

On the level of personal narrative we have two storytellers whose methods and goals appear to be dead ends. Kay King lies to continue her affair with DiMarco, hardly a laudable goal, and is bad at it, considering that she has had at least three marriages to practice on. Julius, on the other hand, weaves complex tales which mildly entertain his listeners and vastly entertain himself. He creates a past and present for himself, filling in the plot and motivation of his life to fit his situation. While his actions are not as selfish as Kay King's, his stories seem transitory and insubstantial, possibly because the majority of his skill is spent on amusing himself.

The constant interplay between the different types of narrative gives *A Little Romance* a reflexive texture which comments upon both the characters' and our attempts to create and perceive. It invites consideration of the aesthetic process and, by showing us several wrong ways to approach art, suggests that a different perspective is needed to move from the confusing, ineffective experiences of the characters to something more useful and worthwhile.

The second half of the film, which follows the teenage lovers as they realize their dream, offers this new perspective. The one narrative in the film which works is the teenagers' romantic legend concerning the Bridge of Sighs. Unlike Kay King's white lies, Julius's elaborate tales, or DiMarco's epics, their story enriches its audience (in particular, the children since they serve as audience and artist in this case; in general, the film audience). It gives them a stronger relationship than they had before and, equally important, an independent perspective that frees them from some of the limiting attitudes present in the society around them. Their use of the story is also different from the other uses of narrative since they do not manipulate people or attempt to hide a weakness. Instead they adopt the story to help them achieve something they believe valuable. Further, their actions, undertaken for personal reasons, paradoxically affect others. Richard King, for example, after deducing the real reason they have gone to Venice, reasserts himself with his wife and boots out DiMarco. He also becomes a more important force in his stepdaughter's life.

Upon examination, the constituent elements of their story, that which makes the "little romance" an attractive example of narrative art, are independence, awareness, and imagination. The teenagers only create their story when they are independent of the cultural attitudes implicit in romantic legends and the actions of adults which dictate how one should act in a relationship; when they are aware that legends and stories are created by people, not sprung self-existent with the force of law from some mysterious source; and when, moving past rational analysis, they imaginatively test the ideas inherent in those cultural myths against their own beliefs and perceptions. They discover that narratives have power because people willingly believe in them, and, armed with that knowledge, select a story that fills their particular needs rather than relying on a well-worn tale.

The implications for the viewer are clear; true narrative requires interaction between artist and audience, and engages rather than manipulates the listener. There is an awareness by both audience and artist of the methods and purposes involved, and a willingness to examine the ideas contained in the narrative. The work exists only when the viewer understands and integrates it into his life. Hill develops this new understanding of narrative through the conventional romance. The obstacles the children encounter, and their efforts to overcome them, are structured to lead to a consideration of aesthetic, as well as spiritual romances.

As the second half of the film begins, the adolescents, despite their accord on sex, still do not have a completely satisfying relationship. They are separated by Lauren's mother, and Lauren is saddened by the knowledge that she will soon return to the United States. In an attempt to salvage something of her love for Daniel, she turns to Julius's legend about the Bridge of Sighs and convinces Daniel to run away with her to Venice. This plan starts out as an adventure, a solution to Lauren's problem, but quickly becomes complicated by jealousy, another unarticulated and often misunderstood aspect of human relationships. They must enlist Julius's help to make their plan work, but the longer he stays with them the more sullen and possessive Daniel becomes. He irrationally regards Julius as a threat to supplant him in Lauren's affections, and his jealousy reaches such a pitch that it affects his feelings for her.

This possessiveness, the attempt to control Lauren's life, is subliminally present in the original meeting with Julius. Lauren finds the old man entertaining, but Daniel is distinctly unimpressed, not only, one suspects, because he is less susceptible to stories, but also because Julius interferes with his attempt to know Lauren. As the attachment grows, so does Daniel's concern for her, and this is apparent in the skirmish with DiMarco. There, Daniel is playing the hero and protecting her against the fop's insinuations, but later his motives are not so pure. At the race track, when Julius's hunch appears to triumph over Daniel's system, the boy turns sulky and threatens to leave; only Lauren's coaxing brings him back into the plan. When Julius's absentmindedness leaves them stranded and penniless at the border, Daniel again becomes sullen and complaining. The trip has become, for him, a contest for Lauren's affections, and he is determined to disgrace Julius. His opportunity finally comes at Verona. The escape by bicycle is a physical test, the one realm in which Daniel has an edge over the adult, and he leaves the old man far behind. Again, only Lauren brings him back, but Daniel is far from repentant. He gloats over Julius's defeat and delights in exposing him as a thief and his stories as "damned lies."

Daniel, who is caught up in film fantasies, suddenly revels in the role of realist. When Julius admits that Emmaline, the supposed inspiration of his life, is "a fantasy," Daniel retorts that "she's a lie." When Julius pleads he was only attempting "to bring a little romance" into his life, Daniel sneers, "that's pretty sad." Accepting only existential evidence, Daniel exposes Julius by revealing the flimsiness of his fictions. Now the victor, Daniel is content to turn back. After all, they have had their fun, Verona was good enough for Romeo and Juliet, and getting to Venice was not that important anyway. Enraptured by his rival's defeat, he hardly cares that the adventure is at an end.

His position, however, is unrealistic. The collapse of the plan is more than a sign to turn back; it is the make or break point for Lauren and Daniel. They are at odds with each other, their adventure is stymied, and their earlier happiness has evaporated with the romantic legend. Lauren, who was completely dependent on the old man's story, now has nothing left to believe in. Daniel, who ardently tried to fulfill the requirements of his movie-inspired fantasies, has gained only a pyrrhic victory. By following the conventional wisdom of their culture, the lovers have boxed themselves in a corner from which there seems to be no escape.

Yet disaster is avoided when Julius points out, and they accept, a different perspective on their situation. He first counters Daniel's criticism that stories are false and "damned lies" by pointing out that legends have a basis in human action. "What are legends anyway," he asks, "but stories of ordinary people doing extraordinary things." It is not the fictions that are important, but the use we make of them.

Laurence Olivier in A Little Romance *struggles with a bicycle and advises the lovers (Diane Lane and Thelonious Bernard).*
(Courtesy: Museum of Modern Art/Film Stills Archive)

Everyone creates narratives, or lies, or in some way tries to shape or escape from the world about them. The secret is to create or select fictions that have meaning for them, and then work to make the dream a reality. "You could make it [the legend] true," he says. "It takes courage and imagination," but "something that two people create together, against impossible odds, can hold them together, forever." In opposition to Daniel's realism, Julius offers a spiritual power that can effect changes beyond physical or intellectual capabilities.

His simple statement serves as a revelation for the group. Daniel relents, Lauren is given new hope, and the trio sets off for Venice. This time the legend of the kiss under the Bridge of Sighs is not something external, a mechanism to provide happiness, but is instead something personal that has a special meaning for them. With a clear understanding of the nature and importance of their goal, they manage to outwit the police, overcome the unscrupulous gondolier, and realize their dream. Even though Lauren leaves for America, it appears their relationship will endure for some time.

Julius's advice is also, obviously, the solution to the problem of narrative raised earlier in the film, for the discussion of romantic legends applies to all kinds of storytelling. Julius's comments point out that the response to a narrative must fall between Daniel's insistence on realism and Lauren's unquestioning belief. In its place there must be a consciousness of the fiction, and then the attempt, through the imagination (since reason always points out the "damned lies"), to integrate that fiction into one's life. As Julius says, it is through the listener's courage and imagination that a narrative takes on life.

By showing us the destruction of the children's illusions and their response, Hill allows us to see the importance of imaginative involvement in the aesthetic experience. The unthinking production of and the uncritical response to art limit both artist and audience; nothing new can be exchanged and the old stories gradually lose their meaning or relevance. Instead of repeating the formulaic stories that have become part of our cultural thinking, the artist must use his imagination to give these stories new life in such a way that the audience is involved with ideas as well as entertained. For their part, the audience must avoid conventional interpretations and test the ideas against their own perceptions.

Thus, when Lauren and Daniel reject the old romantic legends (Daniel is no longer satisfied to stop with what was good enough for Romeo and Juliet) and adopt their own variation, they escape the

need to fulfill formulas or act out particular roles. With a new awareness of the world, they can direct their energy to achieving something
they believe beneficial. Through imagination, they can create a vision
free of the traps which have ensnared DiMarco, Kay King, and
Natalie.

Hill's film is a clear example of a narrative that follows the
guidelines established within the film. He shows us how romances,
both spiritual and aesthetic, are developed and take on meaning; he
also asks the viewer to make a judgment on his narrative rather than
trying to elicit a stock response. In sharing his assumptions and ideas
with us, and in making us partners in the exploration of the subject,
Hill goes beyond the substanceless lozenges usually churned out by
Hollywood. If his film succeeds it is because the viewer understands
and accepts the premises of the story, and, like the adolescents,
chooses to believe in the possibility of love.

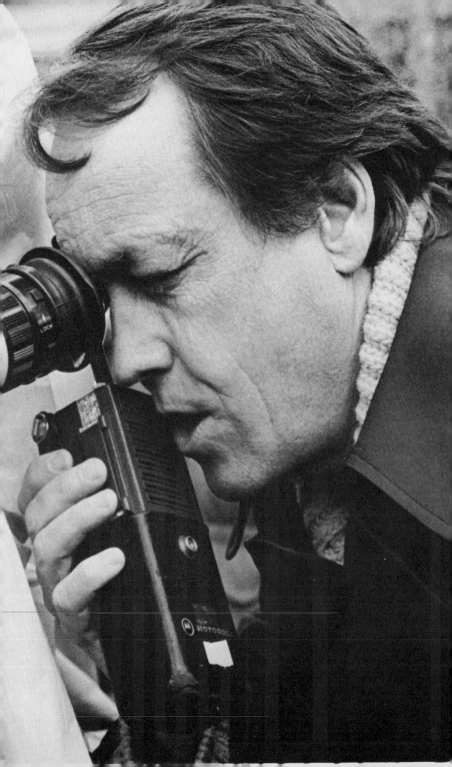

8

A Critique of
American Social Customs

IN REVIEWING Hill's work, one can see that the films are not only cohesive, focused individual works, but that as a group they form a loosely structured critique of American social customs that is greater than the sum of its parts. Through exploration of his chosen subjects and themes, Hill invariably reveals how unthinkingly accepted social beliefs limit, even destroy the individual; he constantly questions, in effect, the conventional perception of the world as an ordered, comprehensible place. Hill's work is not, however, a consciously formulated tract that dogmatically shows the corruption and decay of the American way of life. In his films, Hill emphasizes the tension that exists between two different viewpoints, the desire for individual freedom and the demands of a conformist society. He shows these contradictory impulses locked in a struggle, but, instead of providing a solution to the conflict or the reconciliation typical of conventional efforts, his films depict the complexity and the radicalness of the situation. His work clarifies the problem to increase our understanding, but seldom argues for a particular alternative point of view.

Irony is, as I have suggested, the major tool of Hill's analysis. This irony is not cynicism; Hill is not ironic in every film, nor is he negative for its own sake. Rather, it is indicative of his sensitivity to the complexity of his subjects. The extent to which Hill's vision goes beyond the conventional can be seen through an examination of the conflict between the individual and society, the basic situation upon which Hill's films are built, and the ways in which it is presented in his work.

Individualism, the cornerstone of American society, the mark of national character which we use to differentiate ourselves from other cultures, takes on shadings antithetical to those found in the usual popular presentation of it. Individuals are no longer the trailblazers for the social group, the models who show the mass the right way to live; instead, individuals are not only outside the social group, irrevocably cut off from it, but in that self-willed exile have lost their grasp on the traditional meaning of individualism without finding an acceptable, sustaining substitute. Whereas the classic American individual exhibits self-reliance, rectitude, strength in adversity, concern for others, and use of his skills to further the aims of the social group, Hill's characters are often marked by a narrowness of interest and a distrust of the mass. The sacred link that once existed between the hero and his followers has been broken.

Butch and Sundance, for example, are more properly self-indulgent, affable losers than the last remnants of a dying breed or an expression of individualism. They cannot become the heroes they wish to be because they have no goal other than maintaining their carefree life-style. They have cut themselves off from the spiritless society that is advancing westward, but they have retreated into a solipsistic world that is as enervating as the one they have rejected. Waldo Pepper is another character who has no clear idea of the nature of heroism. He knows he wants to be separate from the mundane world of middle America, but he conceives of individualism—his supposed route of escape—as money and status, the foundations of the society he wishes to leave behind. He nonetheless plunges forward in pursuit of his goal, and in his blindness destroys others and nearly himself before he gains some understanding of his real situation. Reggie Dunlop is another soul who aligns himself with individualism and honor, but whose life is, despite his best efforts and intentions, a parody of the qualities to which he aspires. Reggie's second-class existence is light years away from the idyllic world of sport commended in popular culture, and he is unaware of how shallow, mercenary, and egotistical he has become in the quest for stardom. His callous manipulation of the players and fans, his selfish actions with his wife and Lily Braden, and his succumbing to the lure of glory are evidence that Reggie can never reach the individualism he so desperately wants. The con men in *The Sting* are yet another example of those who have declared their independence from the ordinary world—both of bourgeois citizenry and Lonnegan's monolithic crime machine—and yet end up as models of the rejected society. In their own eyes, the con men are picaresque rogues who define themselves through their manipulative skills, and whose moral code separates them from bullies like Doyle Lonnegan. Ultimately, however, they are as corrupt, as vicious, and as self-concerned as Lonnegan, and the piety of their motive, the justification for the lapses from the moral code, only faintly hides the similarity.

In addition to a false sense of freedom, the characters' adherence to what is perceived as individualism often leads to problems. Butch and Sundance, Waldo Pepper, and Reggie Dunlop are either destroyed or lost because they insist on striving for the idealized version of individualism enshrined by the conventional society. Billy Pilgrim is an analogous case. He clings to another American dream, that of the perfect family, with a tenacity that is obsessive, particularly in light of evidence to the contrary. Since he can never reconcile his unhappy life with the cultural fables, he slips off into the dead-end fantasy of Tralfamadore. In Hill's films, individualism is a pose, not a possibility. The characters have so blindly accepted the stereotypical interpretations of individualism (or the family, or romance) that they do not see how empty the concepts have become or to what paltry ends they have been put.

Yet Hill's attacks on the falseness of the popular conception of individualism are counterbalanced by his genuine appreciation of the individual and his contempt for the social group. Hill likes individuals; he identifies with those who attempt to go beyond the ordinary and resist the pull of the anonymous crowd; and consequently his characters, flawed as they are, are still the central focus of his films, and have enough energy, skill, and virtue to draw audiences to them. We empathize with the characters because they are more noble, intelligent, generous, alert, etc., than the characters in the world around them. Their distancing from the social group is based on a recognition of some flaw in that group, and their rebellions are against an enemy with which the average viewer can easily identify: a depersonalized, rule-bound, confining, timid society that seems too large an opponent for one person to cope with. Butch and Sundance have far more going for them than the dim-witted members of their gang or the lemminglike townspeople; their ingenuity, their concern for each other, and their nearly successful insistence that there is more to life than conformity endear them to us. For most viewers, the virtues eclipse the flaws. Billy Pilgrim, despite his shortcomings, is easily the most attractive character in *Slaughterhouse-Five*. He is kind, generous, forgiving—far more so than his insipid wife, the vicious Lazzaro, or the nonentities of Ilium, and his happiness on Tralfamadore seems a small reward for the suffering he endures. Most viewers grant him his fantasy because it is one of their own. Reggie Dunlop and Waldo

Pepper are also attractive characters, gifted in ways their fellows are not, and their efforts to maintain the integrity of certain verities are understandably attractive. The teenagers in *A Little Romance* are winning, not only because of their youth and intelligence, but because their dream of pure love stands in marked contrast to the spiritless world of the adults around them.

Social groups, on the other hand, are almost always negative in Hill's work. The crowd in *Butch Cassidy* is merely lazy and cowardly, but the crowds in *Slapshot* and *Waldo Pepper* are exemplars of the worst traits in human nature: cowardice, morbid curiosity, mindlessness, indulgence in the most visceral emotions, and meek submission to the group. The prevailing social climate is depersonalized and regimented, a threat that stalks Hill's individuals at every turn.

Yet it is not a simple polarity, a black hats-white hats plot device. Hill recognizes that while individuals may have severed themselves from the crowd they are in actuality still tied to it. As he told me (see the following interview), "they would much rather be with the crowd than be right." Although they might deny it, the characters' dreams are usually identical to those of the existing culture. "We could be heroes," Butch says, and unconsciously speaks for all of Hill's protagonists. By that he means realization of some cultural fantasy and through that achievement some identifiable form of success. It may be money or status, or just differentiation of one's self from the mass, but, whatever its form, it is still the old culture's dream.

His characters fail because they make a crucial mistake. They see that there is a lack of opportunity to realize their dreams in the society around them, or an opposition to those dreams, and they assume that the problem is one of space. Like Butch, always in search of an El Dorado, Hill's characters believe that they only need a new arena in which to operate in order to reach their goals: Billy Pilgrim has Tralfamadore, Daniel and Lauren have Venice, the con men have the subculture of crime, and Waldo Pepper has flying. It usually does not occur to them that there might be something wrong with the dream, that what is needed is not physical separation but a new understanding of the world. Rather than develop a new perspective, they strive to reach the perfect place, and unconsciously mimic the old culture.

It might seem that realization of the group's dreams would be encouraged, that society would want people to prove the validity of its myths, but in Hill's films there is a suggestion that the characters' ardent striving toward a goal is unacceptable. The crowds in *Butch Cassidy* want nothing of qualities like honor, self-reliance, self-respect; they want comfort, and in return for security let others

(Harriman's posse) handle civic responsibilities. The crowds in *Waldo Pepper* and *Slapshot* have given up the chase for glory and have settled instead for vicarious pursuit or indulgence of the emotions through passive attendance at spectacles. Like Jim Carr of *Slapshot*, Lauren's mother in *A Little Romance*, and Dillhoefer and Werfel in *Waldo Pepper*, the members of society brand their world a model of excellence and guard against any evidence that their understanding is false. A character's realization of one of the cultural myths would illustrate the poverty of the existing situation and is thus as threatening to them as revolution. Harriman and the new society deny even the small freedoms of Butch and Sundance; Val, Lazzaro, and the people of Ilium make Billy conform to the stereotyped American dream, denying or suppressing his memories of Dresden; Newton Potts regards Waldo as misguided and Werfel dismisses his concern for historical accuracy as mere pettiness; Jim Carr becomes violent in response to Ned Braden's nonconformance; and Kay King overreacts to her daughter's innocent relationship out of an unreasoned fear: they intuitively know that realization of the dream, or an achievement of the goal without the promised rewards, would invalidate the basis of their existence.

Thus Hill's films are primarily negative in tone, for he has not yet found an easy road out of this situation. Occasionally his characters reach an understanding of their lives (as in *Waldo Pepper*), or (as in *A Little Romance*) gain an insight that helps them overcome their problems, but Hill is not yet such an optimist that he can give the audience that message of hope, of a world benevolently ordered, typical of the conventional movie. His next film, *The World According to Garp*, would seem in keeping with this outlook since it is like *Slaughterhouse-Five* or *Waldo Pepper* in that opportunities for optimism, despite the humor, are minimal. In Hill's filmic world the individual's struggle for accommodation with the social group does not yet admit a solution.

A second interesting feature of Hill's work is the concern with art and the artist. Although it may not be as conscious a part of the films as the focus on the individual, it is nonetheless an important element of his work; use of the imagination or manipulative ability is as essential to defining character as are attitudes and actions. Typically, Hill's presentation of art is not settled into a predictable pattern. Ideally, art organizes and makes experience comprehensible, and the artist transmits the vision to the social group; in Hill's films, art has no redemptive or organizing power. Instead, we see a debased form of art in which the artist has become the con artist, satisfied with conjurer's illusions instead of the fictions that illuminate the lives of his audience. The goal of artistic effort is no longer enlightenment of the group, or even self-advancement, but has become self-satisfaction. There are phony artists who proclaim their sanctity in an attempt to aggrandize themselves (Werfel in *Waldo Pepper*, DiMarco in *A Little Romance*, and Henry Orient), and there are con artists (the con men in *The Sting*, Reggie Dunlop, Julius in *A Little Romance*, and Butch). They "create" worlds to achieve specific ends, and must keep their audience unenlightened, trapped in the illusion, to reach their goals. Gondorff and Hooker must keep Lonnegan's con in order to make the sting work; Werfel, Dillhoefer, DiMarco, and Henry Orient keep up the facade of presenting the real thing in order to dupe the public. Butch keeps Sundance and himself going with stories of Australia and Bolivia; and Lauren, Daniel, and Julius all hide behind fictions to keep the world from discovering their problems. Reggie can never let his players in on the Florida-sale plan because the loss of the dream would destroy the team. When he does tell them, the team collapses into incompetence and is revived only when a new dream (the attendance of the NHL scouts and possible pro contracts) inspires them. Billy Pilgrim is a clear case of someone inhabiting a self-created fantasy; he can never admit Tralfamadore is a dream without destroying himself.

The portrayal of art is not, however, entirely negative; occasionally in Hill's work the artistic process becomes a means of liberating the characters. Waldo Pepper uses the props of a Hollywood movie production to create the dream world he has so long cherished, and realization of that dream gives him an understanding of himself and society that has been denied him by the other artifacts of his culture. Moreover, Waldo's aesthetic, if you will, is different from the typical examples of popular culture. Waldo recreates the World War I experience to understand it; there is no pandering to the lowest taste or self-glorification, nor is there an attempt to manipulate the emotions of people. He shows us that there is another aspect to artistic endeavor that, while apparently in eclipse, is not completely lost. The two teenagers in *A Little Romance* are similar. They create their own legend of romance, divesting themselves of the culture's readily available myths, and in so doing find the love for which they have been searching. Once they reject the old ways of seeing, they gain important insights into themselves, the nature of romance, and even the nature of social myths. They also show the audience that fiction making can serve other ends than that of entertainment.

Once again, as with the studies of the individual, there is a sense of possibility in Hill's work that gives it an additional dimension not often found in commercial cinema. He is not frozen into ambivalence, lapsed into superior knowledge, or content with negativism. He is still on a voyage of discovery, and in addition to the narrative sense, the technical skill, and the understanding of characters that makes his films popular, there is an intelligence and vision in his work that assures us both the journey and the destination are worthwhile.

I MET WITH George Roy Hill at his New York office in December, 1980, and then talked with him later by phone. He was then busy preparing John Irving's best-selling novel *The World According to Garp* for production, but graciously took time from his schedule to talk about his films.

EFS: It seems, in watching your films, that there are a number of themes that you come back to: the emptiness of success, for example, or the hollowness of cultural beliefs about the individual or the family. Your characters are similar, too, in that they all have a dream which they struggle to attain and which, when they get it, doesn't satisfy them at all.

GRH: I feel unmasked. I spent a good part of my career trying to make it appear that I was doing as wide a variety of things as one could possibly do. In fact, I was doing pretty much the same things over and over again. One thing, for example, that they never uncovered was that *A Little Romance* is practically a remake of *Henry Orient*.

EFS: I noticed that. The two girls even share a love of Elizabeth Barrett Browning.

GRH: That's right. And the mother is a tramp carrying on with a phony. But they have the dream, they have the fantasy, they build a dream around something that's in the future, and then it all crumbles in the end.

EFS: I noticed that you had a slightly different resolution to *A Little Romance*. When Val Boyd of *Henry Orient* loses her fantasy, she's pretty much lost until her father comes back—

GRH: But the father in *A Little Romance* is very much the same father as the father in *Henry Orient*.

EFS: It seems as if the dream of the child inspires the father. When the father realizes that Lauren has run away with Daniel he decides to go to her, and he kicks out DiMarco.

131

GRH: DiMarco out as Sellers was kind of bounced in *Henry Orient*. [*Pauses*] I know you start your dissertation on me after *Thoroughly Modern Millie*. Actually, the theme that I was working on—which is the, not the shallowness of the American dream—I can't put it in so many words—but the minister in *Hawaii* is certainly one who took the American dream to that island and destroyed everybody in the process.

EFS: Unintentionally, but effectively.

GRH: I was really trying to make an anti-Vietnam movie.

EFS: At that time? Really?

GRH: I was violently anti-Vietnam very, very early. It was really a deliberate effort, and again nobody saw it as a plea for us not to transfer our values—which aren't all that hot anyway—into another society which had a perfectly good set of values of their own. And by enforcing our values or imposing them on the Hawaiian society, we destroyed them.

EFS: I remember reading that that was Michener's concept, but I don't think he ever saw it as applicable to anything outside of that one story.

GRH: No, I don't think he did either. I talked with Michener and I told him that I was going to try to make it anti-Vietnam and he was very pleased with it. But that had such an ugly history of production. I was fired off it twice—three times—and I quit once. So I spent too much of my time fighting the office battles and that didn't leave me enough time to do the picture the way I really wanted to do it.

EFS: What did they want? More action?

GRH: They wanted a historical romance. It kind of fell between what I wanted and what they wanted.

EFS: Did you have any trouble with any of your other films?

GRH: No. That was enough trouble for all my films. I had trouble on *Thoroughly Modern Millie* after the film was shot. I handed in a cut of it that was fifteen to twenty minutes shorter than the cut that they released. But they liked it so much—and those were the days when they thought a road show with an intermission would bring more money—so they took twenty minutes of that film and put it back in and then put an intermission in . . . But when they put the intermission in, it was like taking a souffle out of the oven to look at it halfway through.

EFS: When you started out you were in theater, weren't you? And you did television as well.

GRH: I did a lot of TV. I did the original *Judgment at Nuremburg* on television. I did *A Night to Remember,* which was the sinking of the *Titanic,* which was a live production, and a tremendous production. I think it was the most complicated live production that was ever done, and it was very successful. They have a copy of it, I think, at the Museum of Modern Art. I did *Oh Child of Our Times*, which was a political piece. I did *Last Clear Chance* with Paul Muni. I did several—I did an awful lot—I must have done fifty television shows, which is where I learned my craft.

EFS: And did you do theater at the same time?

GRH: Yes. I did *Look Homeward, Angel* on Broadway. I did a lot of things: *Moon on a Rainbow Shawl, Gang's All Here,* Frank Loesser's *Greenwillow*—

EFS: You were working every day.

GRH: Oh yes, I've been working hard. But I haven't—one of the things that I've been very careful about is publicity. I don't like publicity. I don't like to give interviews and I haven't. I've given one interview, really, for the *New York Times Magazine.*

EFS: There's not a great deal written on you.

GRH: Well, that's deliberate. I keep my own private life as private as I possibly can and I won't even let them release pictures of me on the film's publicity. I find publicity is distasteful and I don't think it does the picture any good to focus on the director. I think it's only a very small group of the public that really pays attention to the director. Lately it's come around so that the director is more of a star than he was, but I've never wanted that. I feel that I can accomplish more if I have a low profile, and my profile in the business is just fine, I mean, in the business where it counts.

EFS: What did you see in the opportunity to work in films that really made you feel you could stop working in the theater?

GRH: In the theater the vision, in order for it to be really successful, has to be the writer's. He has full control; you can't cut words—you can't by contract—you can't touch a thing he says. In the film, the director has that control. You can shape a piece according to your own vision. You can't on the stage. Also you need, not better actors, but more accomplished—technically—actors on the stage. If you have a scene up there that's not working, you can't cut around, you can't get the camera off somebody when they're not doing so well and shape it so that you can protect them. Those actors are up there on their own and just doing their best. I've sat in the back of theater many times and thought, "God damn it, if I had that on film I'd just cut that." I would go around and I'd get a close up of this and I'd be able to say it all with looks, and you wouldn't have to go through it. You just have infinitely more control.

EFS: Are there any directors you admire today?

GRH: The directors I really admire—I think Milos Forman is probably the best director working today. He's tremendous. He directs with such style and such insight.

EFS: Do you go to movies a lot?

GRH: No. It's very hard to go to movies where you can relax and enjoy. You're watching all the time. I will keep up on movies by, say, coming to New York for a month and having films run for me and going to where I can see two movies a day. I'll go for a week or two weeks to see movie after movie. But I don't normally go to movies on a regular basis.

EFS: Are there any directors that you like besides Milos Forman? Any among the young American directors?

GRH: I think George Lucas's *American Graffiti* was a brilliant piece of work, but George doesn't want to direct. I thought *American Graffiti* was one of the best jobs of directing actors that I'd ever seen. I was very disappointed when he went on and became a tycoon. Coppola, I thought, did a marvelous job with *Godfathers I and II*. I just thought he did a splendid job. I think a lot of them are technically superior to most of us—they've gone to film school, they know the cameras, they know the stocks, they know technically how to make things work. But I find them, generally speaking, with some excep-tions, rather not as good with performers, with actors.

EFS: What about Europeans?

GRH: I have trouble with European films because I don't under-stand them; I mean, I don't understand the language. I like Truffaut's work. I loved *Day for Night*. It's a marvelous film. It's the kind of film I would have liked to have had made myself. But Bergman—some of his early films I like enormously; I loved *Virgin Spring*. I loved the work that Tony Richardson did in *Taste of Honey* and *The Long Distance Runner*. I don't know what's happened to Tony. He doesn't seem to be doing the kind of thing that he did before, but I admired him a great deal.

EFS: Any cross-pollinization there?

GRH: It's funny. For example, when Vincent Canby was damning *Butch Cassidy* he said it was a rip-off on *Jules and Jim*. I had not seen *Jules and Jim*. I can see why he would have thought so, but it was kind of a stretch even then. . . .

EFS: One thing I found running through your films is artist figures. I noticed many of your characters try to create a specific environment and try to control that environment. Is there anything to that observation, or is it just something I've put in there?

GRH: Well, I'll tell you the truth; I never thought of it in those terms. But let me see if that's something I may have been thinking of subconsciously. Maybe, again, that's the kind of a character that would appeal to me—and I never analyze why the people appeal to me in intellectual terms. You have the two little girls in *Henry Orient* creating the myth of Henry Orient, the man that they love and how sensitive he is; they create a myth. And you have the boy and the girl in *A Little Romance* who create a myth and then live up to it. We have Waldo, of course, who is trying to recreate [the past]. We have Reggie Dunlop. We have the dreaming of Butch and Sundance, and they're talking about their future myth about living in Australia when they're helping each other die. God, again I feel embarrassed because you seem to have found a thread that has never been a conscious thread of mine, because I haven't done that consciously. I haven't said I'm going to create people who create their own environment.

EFS: In *The Sting* you can really see the creation of this environment. They have a meeting to set up the plan—

GRH: Oh, you have an elaborate environment in *The Sting*.

EFS: They create a set; they rent props. You see a guy come in with a suitcase who says "Me specialty is an Englishman."

GRH: Tom Spradley.

EFS: Then there's a shot of him putting makeup on the Erie Kid's nose. There are shots of people milling about like extras, waiting to go on. It seems that these people are setting up a production.

GRH: Absolutely.

EFS: It seems your other characters are like that too. Reggie's a manipulator, although he doesn't like what he creates. When he hears Killer Carlson on the radio he says, "What a nightmare!"

GRH: [*Laughs*] Well, things are getting out of hand. When he sees Braden on the ice doing the striptease he recognizes it for what it is and he says, "Right on, right on, you finally caught on. I don't care if you're a fighter or if you have to do a striptease, you're pleasing the audience."

EFS: I notice that many of your artist figures fail. The con men in *The Sting*, for example, set out to avenge Luther, but in the end it seems as if they do it as much for fun as anything. That's a real shift.

GRH: Hooker says, "You're right; it wasn't enough; it was close." Of course, Gondorff has told him from the beginning that he has to keep the guy's con in order to make it work. He's never going to be told that he was taken. So the revenge is kind of—not as satisfying as it might be if the man knew that he had been taken, but he doesn't know it. So it's a kind of a sad—and that's why Hooker doesn't take the money. The money meant nothing to him—so it's a very unsatisfying revenge.

EFS: I think that's important, because most people assume it's just entertainment. But when I saw it the ending bothered me, and the beginning bothered me. I wondered why you put yourself in those titles.

GRH: Well, I wanted to stress two things. One was the fact that it was a confection, or an invention. I had David Ward in it, and Newman and Redford standing in that one scene. Then I had Bob Shaw in back of them. Then I pulled back farther in the drawing and saw myself—or was David next, I've forgotten—but David, I think, was next. Also I wanted to say this is a *Saturday Evening Post* serial. I got Henry Bumstead to do all the sets in the roto gravure color of the *Saturday Evening Post*. We used more browns in that thing. Then I introduced all the characters in the beginning of the film as they were done in the thirties, showing little bits of them acting. But I did that for a specific reason. I was so afraid that we wouldn't be able to pull the con off on the audience that I had Dana Elcar—who played the [pretended] FBI man—and I put him down as "FBI Agent Polk." So that subliminally when you saw his picture up there you read "FBI Agent Polk"—and that nailed him as an FBI agent, and that's the only cheat that I did in the whole thing. [Hill's point is that the audience is led to believe by the titles that one of the con men is actually a federal agent.]

EFS: One thing that I thought could be a cheat was the shot of Loretta Sallino at the cash register, smiling after Hooker has already gone. I thought, "She's the love interest."

GRH: That's not a cheat. She could be smiling at him; no, I won't accept that as a cheat. I'll accept FBI Agent Polk as a cheat.

EFS: It just seemed we weren't clued in on her as we were with most of the other subplots, like the scam at the Western Union office.

GRH: The clue I gave you, which I was debating putting in or leaving out, was when—and this was a big clue—when Redford was getting ready for the final sting, and he takes the capsule out and he opens it and he puts it back together again. What the audience thought he was doing, I don't know, but if you see the film the second time you knew he was preparing the blood capsule. So I felt I was rather daring on that.

EFS: It seems most of your characters have a hard time working things out. These guys in *The Sting* don't achieve their goal. Waldo comes to an understanding of his situation, and then drifts off into the clouds. Poor Reggie never escapes—

GRH: No, but as I say, Reggie has that moment of understanding.

EFS: The kids in *A Little Romance* seem positive because they seem to know that, well, the romantic myths are just old legends they've been given, it's just made up.

GRH: Then they make it real.

EFS: It's like Laurence Olivier says, "It's not the legend, it's your courage and imagination, your willingness to believe."

GRH: Well, again they create their own environment, but they do it positively; it's a more positive ending than I usually have.

EFS: Yes, that's what I found. What will *Garp* be like?

GRH: In *Garp*, I'm having a baby in the opening of the film—if I can shoot it properly—having the baby come up just into a blue frame, just up to about the eyes and then down. And then up again a little farther and he's looking out into the world, and then he gets up a little farther and he looks out and sees it's good. Then I sail him through the frame. You wouldn't think I'd be able to get flying into *Garp*, but I do. The opening of *Garp* is curiously a little like the little boy in *Waldo Pepper*. It's a flying dream. In fact, I was going to do the opening of *Waldo Pepper* the way I'm going to do *Garp*, with a boy flying through the air. Now I have a naked child flying through the air. And at the end of the film, if I do it the way I'm planning on doing it, he's—Garp is obsessed by flying—

EFS: Really?

GRH: Yes [*laughs*], I've kind of injected my own themes into *Garp* that way. In the end, when he's in a helicopter being taken away after he's been shot, and after the helicopter goes up I'm going to bring that child back again. So it's a cyclical thing, and it comes back to the life, the whole life.

EFS: I don't know if you ever consider it or not, but do you worry about the public's expectations? *Garp* was such a monstrous success as a book that it seems natural people will expect certain things from it.

GRH: Can't worry about it. I can't even think about it. Obviously I hope the film reaches a wide audience. As Garp says in the film—I have him say in the film—"I don't care about critics." Because he's been praised by critics. He says, "I don't want critics, I want an audience, a big audience." You want to get your stuff out there so people can see it. Whether you're praised or condemned by critics doesn't make any difference because critics change; there's always a revisionist view. And also, you spend your life hearing about the great artists who never were understood in their lifetime, and it seems to me that contemporary critics have been historically more wrong than they've been right. Even Mozart suffered a great loss of popularity at the end of his life. Van Gogh didn't sell a picture before he died. So that's why if you have a historical perspective, you can see why you don't really care about critics. All you want is enough money to buy your paints and your canvases. And although it's a little more expensive than paint or canvases in Hollywood, it's still basically the same thing. If you've got the ability to get the wherewithall to make the films, that's what counts, not the critics. . . .

EFS: One thing I'd like to talk about is the music in your films. It seems to be a very important part of all that you do, and I guess the most famous example is *The Sting*. How did that come about?

GRH: I scored the whole movie with records, with Joshua Rifkin records and Gunther Schiller's arrangements before Marvin got a hold of it. I have a very strong musical background and I usually pick out the music for my films before I do anything with a film.

EFS: Why did you pick out Scott Joplin? As has been pointed out, he's not contemporary with that period.

GRH: No, he isn't. Curiously enough I picked Scott Joplin before I even cast the film. I picked him because I was working on the script and I went up to my brother's house in Oakland, and his son was playing the piano, and playing some Joplin rags, and I sat down and we spent a whole afternoon, his son and I, going through the rags. By the time I finished, I knew exactly the ones I wanted to use and exactly what parts of the movie—and that was before I even cast it.

EFS: Just a fortuitous accident.

GRH: Yes, and David Ward was deeply upset that I was going to use it because he wanted—and he indicated in the script—that he wanted the blues, the authentic blues of that period, which would have been much more representative of the period and location, Chicago. But those blues—while I love those blues—did not have the flavor, the kind of game flavor, that I wanted to have as a background for the picture. Although I know it was absolutely anachronistic, it still gave the result that I wanted.

EFS: What about *Slapshot*? There you seem to use the music thematically. I'm thinking of the American flag and the national anthem at the beginning and at the end, if I remember correctly, the band closes out with "I'm a Yankee Doodle Dandy."

GRH: Yes, I used all the band music that they played. It was very American. Did you like the fact that all the generals were lined up in front of *Deep Throat*?

EFS: No, I didn't see that.

GRH: In the parade, in the reviewing stand, right in front of the theater there that was playing *Deep Throat*. [*Laughs*] How American can you get?

EFS: One thing I wanted to ask you about was the genres that you've worked in. You've done a Western, a big caper film, an antiwar film, and a sports film. The one thing I haven't seen out of you in a number of years is a love story, an adult love story. Is it that there's no market? No script?

GRH: Well, I was looking for a love story, and wanted desperately to do a love story, when I came across the French book $E = mc^2$, *Mon Amour*, which I made *A Little Romance* from. It just seemed the kind of love story I wanted to tell couldn't be told about anybody except those kids. I wanted to do a love story, but again whatever it is that attracts me to things brought me right back to that old theme of *Henry Orient* and those two kids. So I did that; I was more comfortable with it.

EFS: You're sometimes accused of starting the buddy films.

GRH: Oh, of course, that's nonsense. They had buddy films long before that. They had Tracy and Gable, and Pat O'Brien and James Cagney.

EFS: The complaint was that there were no films that dealt with adult women, not even in a love story.

GRH: The first film, *Period of Adjustment*, was a love story, and *Thoroughly Modern Millie* was kind of a fun love story. But it's not a subject—my instinct is to approach things, I think, in a much more lighthearted way than a serious, agonizing way—I don't want to do Tristan. I don't want to do *Camille*.

EFS: There seems to be a dearth of love stories at the present time.

GRH: I don't know any really good American love stories that I've seen in the last several years. I don't remember good love stories on a serious level. I can remember Astaire and Rogers. The film you were talking about, *It Happened One Night*, was a great love story, but you have to go into European literature. I don't know why Americans are unable to produce really great love stories. I think probably because we've been a nation of action, of expansion, and most of our myths come from the expanding of the country. Women are a bore in

Westerns. From the time I was a child, when the guy hung up his hat and went inside to visit his lady friend, I'd go out for popcorn and come back when the love scene was over. Women stand in the way of action because their role, in our country, has been one of staying at home taking care of the children while the guy's out fighting the Indians. So I don't think we've developed a literature of love stories as much as we've developed a literature of action.

EFS: I noticed in A *Little Romance* one thing that doesn't come up too much in love stories anymore, and that's the question of sex. Whether or not they go to bed seems to be an important issue.

GRH: I made a very deliberate choice not to extend their relationship into a sexual one. They spend the night in Verona together, and one can assume or not assume that they have a sexual experience, but that wasn't what I was aiming for in their relationship. I didn't want to have it. Really, you don't again—in *Tristan and Isolde*, which is probably the greatest love story of all—you don't describe them fucking at all. You just describe their enormous attraction to each other. I was afraid by bringing it into a sexual relationship I would destroy the other relationship, which was much more important. Whether they fucked or not was not that important to me, and it shouldn't have been to them.

EFS: They contrast with the adults in the film, who are simultaneously interested in sex and at the same time suppress the teenagers' interest in sex.

GRH: I know; it's an enormous hypocrisy.

EFS: Your films are usually comedies, but it seems that there's often a darker side to them as well. You often have serious subjects, such as love or the loss of honor or individualism, even though your treatment is humorous.

GRH: I try to cover up my innate pessimism with humor. There are two quotes that have impressed me for a long time. One was a quote of Hugh Walpole's. Let me see, it was "to a thinking man life is comic, and to a feeling man life is tragic." As a matter of fact, I think John Irving used that somewhere in *Garp*. The other quote, which I remember from a long time ago, and I've used it so many times in so many ways I'm sure I'm paraphrasing it terribly, was a George Bernard Shaw quote. He said something like "tears are the natural expression of happiness and laughter is the natural voice of despair."

EFS: That applies to you.

GRH: That's right, and it applies very, very much to my films. I despair through laughter.

EFS: Will that continue? What will *Garp* be like?

GRH: Well, we'll see what happens with *Garp*. It's a real risk, but what the hell. You learn very early in life, in your artistic life, that you're not able to judge what's going to be commercially successful and what isn't going to be commercially successful. I've been very fortunate so far in my films being, for the most part, commercially very successful. But I've also had a lot of flops. Balanced on the one hand with their being successful, my films have generally been scorned by critics, and so that always balances out. You can't tell. There's just no way of knowing. The great thing I've always felt is that it's very important for me to pick my failures, because if I fail I want to fail big, I want to fail attempting something. If I fail by doing things easy or not taking chances, then that's an ignominious failure. Failure is the norm; it's why success is so hard to deal with for a lot of people. They don't realize that the bulk of your work is going to be failure and that the exception is going to be success. You can deal with failure—we can all deal with failure, we're so used to it—but success is very hard to deal with.

EFS: To shift ground again, your films seem to reflect a lot on the creative process. Is that something you do consciously?

GRH: I think it's very dangerous for a creative person to be very analytical about his own creativity. I think that whatever the things are that spur me to do things, and make me take certain projects, have certain visions, is very complicated. I don't want to analyze it; I just want to keep on doing it. I have a very limited span of concentration for self-examination; I don't examine myself at all. . . .

EFS: Let's talk about *Slapshot*. Two criticisms of the film were that the language was excessive, and that sports aren't really that violent, that you exaggerated things.

GRH: One sportsman said the idea of three guys going out on the ice with glasses like that is absolutely ridiculous—well those kids wear those glasses. And they're in that league. I think it's the rage of Caliban looking into the mirror. It took them by surprise, that film.

EFS: It seems people, the fans, have to justify violence; they look at it and call it sportsmanship because they have some sort of need for it.

GRH: And they don't like being laughed at. Nobody gets really badly hurt in *Slapshot*; a guy gets a split lip, that's all. The critics called it ultraviolent and fascist. I mean, they just went—crazy. These critics are the people who would praise *Carrie* and films where these guys' throats are slit, and Peckinpah's violence. It's because they've treated violence as a solemn part of American life, and as long as you do that you can show a guy's head being blown off. But if you laugh at it they become very uptight.

EFS: I noticed that the characters in the film seem to fail as men. They're terrible husbands, and are unable to communicate with women at all, yet they're desperate for the attention of women.

GRH: Yeah, they're a sad bunch. I got very fond of them as a group. They work for so little, and the salaries they get are so small; and the work is so hard, and their active life is so short.

EFS: It seems they're doomed and they don't know they're trapped in that world, and in that way they're like many of your characters: they chase after a dream, but even if they get it they don't see where they've ended up.

GRH: Exactly, or if they do see it is only a momentary flash. It's taking apart, to a certain extent, the success values of our culture.

EFS: Waldo Pepper is a good example of that. He somehow assumes that if he can do the outside loop or meet Kessler that all his problems will be solved. He'll have Maudie, he'll have money.

GRH: Yes, well that's what we're taught. You work hard and accomplish your dream—it doesn't matter what the dream is—it's the tremendous success syndrome. We're all taught to achieve the tremendous success, not knowing that when we do achieve that success it very often turns to ashes.

EFS: Most of your characters never realize that. Butch and Sundance are joking about going to Australia when they die, and they never really see the light. Waldo seems to get a moment of understanding at the end of the film, but then he dies. In this sense, you're somewhat of a pessimist about our culture.

GRH: Well, there's an enormous amount of pessimism in my work. I'm not terribly pleased that you uncovered it. Because, to all intents and purposes, unless you dig at it, I don't think you see it. There's a lot of criticism, but I hope I cover it up with enough humor. My own basic—well, it isn't pessimism. I just think that things are cyclical. I think that there's birth, and regeneration—it's like *Finnegans Wake*, which I studied when I was living in Ireland. It's in Billy Pilgrim when he finally goes off his rocker and lives in the dome, which I furnished as a presidential suite in the Holiday Hotel. That represents the ultimate of what he wants. But even he has—there's a birth, there's a child; life goes on.

EFS: It seems that film is so ironic, and yet it was often praised for being cheerful. We're told this is what we should do, adopt Billy's philosophy.

GRH: [*Laughs*] Concentrate on the good times and ignore the bad.

EFS: One of the things I wanted to ask you is how you're going to do some of the violent scenes in *Garp*. I'm thinking of the crash scene where Duncan loses his eye and Walt is killed. That seems to be a crucial scene, and it seems necessary to capture that kind of violence.

GRH: I'm not going to do it clinically. I'll do it; I'll do everything up to and including the crash, but I don't think I'll show the immediate bloody aftermath. In the book he—John Irving—says it's like a dream, and then cuts to Dog's Head Harbor. So that's what I'm going to do.

EFS: When I read it I thought it would be difficult to film. Many mainstream films are more positive these days than they were in the sixties, and the violence in *Garp* seemed to go against that trend.

GRH: Well, there's violence in it all right, but it needn't be the kind of graphic violence of things like the DePalma film, *Dressed to Kill*. It isn't bloody corpses and slit throats and slashing victims. It isn't that at all. It's a couple of clean deaths with a rifle and one rather nasty accident. It's a very chancy subject; there's no question about it. It's very difficult. It's a big book, and it's a sprawling book, and to try to make a coherent pattern out of it is tough as hell. . . .

EFS: You're one of those directors who uses the same supporting people over and over again. William Reynolds, Henry Bumstead, for example.

GRH: Well, you tend to use the same people, particularly, for example, Bumstead. I've worked with Bumstead for so long that I can send him out location scouting, and he knows my taste so well, that he'll call me and say I've got two houses for you to look at instead of fifty houses. He's a brilliant man. He's probably one of the most underestimated art directors that ever came out of Hollywood. His work on *Slaughterhouse* was just unbelievable.

EFS: That's the one thing I've always wondered about. Where did you find the locale for the bombed-out Dresden?

GRH: We found a town, Most, north of Prague, in Czechoslovakia. They were destroying the town to get at the coal underneath the town. We found it—Bumstead found it, I think—and called me and said come on over here. One good thing about a Communist government is that you go to the head of the government and say "we want to spend some money here and we want to have certain facilities,"—you get them. So we got them to stop the destruction of the town. Then Bumstead went up there and they started destroying it to Bumstead's specifications, leaving the walls standing, the pillars, and all of that. Bumstead spent, oh, a month and a half up there in the coldest weather, building—destroying—that town so it would look like Dresden. And it was magnificent. It was a great piece of work because I didn't have the faintest idea how we were going to do that.

EFS: You wouldn't agree then with the old auteur theory, about the director being the single force behind a picture?

GRH: You know, when you talk about an auteur theory it always bugs me. When I think of, for example, the contributions Bumstead made to that picture. No fucking auteur thought of that town. It was a tremendous addition. And Ondricek's photography was brilliant. Yes, it came through my vision; yes, I worked on the script for four months solid before I even started the picture; and yes, I'm proud it was my vision. But you can't—when you say auteur you're thinking it's author and that it's all his. It isn't all his; it's a collaborative medium.

EFS: In *Butch Cassidy* you seemed to go for a certain visual style; there were a lot of earth tones, an almost monochromatic color. How seriously and thoroughly do you plan that? Did you include the cameraman, Conrad Hall, in your talks?

GRH: Oh you betcha. For example, I put Connie on a month ahead of time and took him on location scouting with me. So we picked the locations together, and we even picked the angles as to where we would shoot to get that kind of shot—where the sun would be, what time of day we'd shoot it. It was all planned out—I'm a fiend on planning—that was all planned out well, well ahead of time.

EFS: Not many directors go that far.

GRH: Well, the work I do in the next four months on *Garp* is going to be down to such detail that when I finally get to rehearsal I've got the whole picture in my head. I've got the shots; I've got the way it's going to be. They're starting construction on the sets next month; meanwhile, I've gone to all the locations; I've picked my shots.

EFS: We talked a little bit earlier about critics and how obtuse they can be when writing about films. Audiences sometimes seem much quicker in catching on to what a film's about.

GRH: Well, that's also a theory of mine. I would much rather play to audiences than critics. The critics can be devastating. They have never ruined a director whom they have disliked, but they have ruined directors that they've liked because they have brought them to the point where—particularly if you're young and impressionable—they put pressure on them as being great artists. So that a poor, young director, who hasn't had that much experience with flops, goes out and says I've got to make this film that the critics will like instead of what the audience will like, and they go down the tubes. Hollywood will do the same thing. Hollywood will give a young director the instrument with which to kill himself: which is absolute money control and an absolute free hand. It's terrible, and then Hollywood will turn on him and not give him a job again. It's a cruel world out there.

EFS: Something like that often happens to actors. If an actor has a flop, people suddenly start saying that he can't act. It's a strange phenomenon.

GRH: Well, it happens with actors, with writers. Steve Tesich was saying the other day—after he had done *Breaking Away* he had this script that the studios had turned down and they were all now anxious to buy. And he said, "What makes that script any better now than when they turned it down?" What it really says to Steve, as he says, is "I've got to be goddamn careful because nobody is putting a rein on me. They're gonna give me enought rope to hang myself" . . .

EFS: We were talking about TV versions of films and how they're cut up. I noticed that the TV version of *Waldo Pepper* didn't have the prologue. To me, that was an important part of the film.

GRH: The whole first part of that was my scrapbook that I kept as a child . . . on Frank Park, Dick Grace, Speed Holman—who was a personal hero of mine, who was in Minneapolis, St. Paul, actually. There's still a Holman field in St. Paul. But I used to watch them as a child and I was—I kept all the scrapbooks about all the pilots and the stunt pilots in Hollywood of that day.

EFS: Were you disappointed with the reaction the film got? I understand it didn't do too well financially.

GRH: Financially it did all right. It didn't do too well critically. But I'll tell you what I was disappointed at. I made a very great mistake in that film and that was by dropping that girl off the wing.

EFS: I know. I remember the times that I saw the film that the audiences were just shocked by that. It seemed to be the point where the mood shifted radically—

GRH: We lost the audience. I know. I turned it—I do that in a lot of my films, but I do it more gracefully than I did it in that. I turned it from fun and games into a darker film because I want to make my point—the point that you talk about—but this was a little too abrupt. Having started it out in great humor and great high jinks and fun and games, I could just feel' that audience—when I took it out on preview—I could just feel that audience sink. In fact, they laughed when Mary Beth first fell off the wing because they knew she'd live. Then they felt betrayed that I'd trapped them into laughing and they felt foolish. I'd done the same thing in *The Sting*, but I'd redeemed them. When Newman killed Redford and then got killed himself—when I took it out on preview I heard people say, "Oh, God, no, oh shit, no, no." But then I made it all right for them.

EFS: When I taught that film, some of my students, who were would-be pilots, loved it. The air sequences were so stunning that they ignored everything else.

GRH: [*Laughs*] Probably just as well. What I did—it's really the wrong way to go about doing a movie. I was a very close friend of Frank Tallman's, the great stunt pilot, who was killed about three years ago, four years ago. Frank and I talked for years about this project, and really what I did was to work out with Frank all the stunts that we could possibly do that would require the kind of skill that he had and then I tried to put a story around it.

EFS: The wrong way to do a film.

GRH: [*Laughs*] The worst way to do a film. So the film exists for those stunts. Those students who were into flying, they were my audience. I just tried to get something to hang on those stuntmen. And there was no process in that film; it was all done for real. Ed Herrmann was in that cockpit when he did the outside loop right over the field. That was Art Scholl who was flying the plane, and ducked down, and the camera was right over his head, and Ed Herrmann's head was right off the ground, about six feet. That takes guts. We were the only major air film that was done that didn't kill somebody.

EFS: Many people have commented on your films and the seeming fascination with the past. Are there any elements of the past that you feel still impinge on the present, still affect people?

GRH: It was somebody else who called me that "Master of Nostalgia" thing. I never thought of myself as somebody who had any particular nostalgia for the past. In fact, I think that there's a kind of, a streak of cynicism in my dealing with themes of the past that I may have disguised. But it certainly isn't that I want to go back to the good old days, because people never came out very well in those good old days either.

EFS: Do you focus on certain cultural legacies, such as codes of honor, or our sense of righteousness, that intrigue you?

GRH: Yes, I know that I like to deal with intangibles—you mentioned codes of honor, behavior, loyalty. Yet my basic work seems to be, as you found out, more pessimistic, taking the American codes and showing how they don't really work in the way that we all imagine. We imagine that if we're good people, and behave well toward our neighbors, and do the right thing, that you'll be happy, and it doesn't work that way.

EFS: One of the more striking contrasts in your work is the difference between individuals and groups of people. You may find flaws with individuals, but you generally seem to like them; but, groups of people always come off badly in your films.

GRH: Well, I've always had a horror of crowds, not wandering in crowds, I don't mind that. Crowd psychology, mob psychology, and mob behavior has always struck me as bringing out the worst in people. They suddenly lose all their standards of individual behavior and, if they can identify themselves with a crowd, all of their individual standards go right down the drain and they become part of a large, howling pack. You wouldn't see one person in an audience—for example, if there was a fight out on the ice—you wouldn't see one person up there screaming, and saying, "Kill him, kill him."

EFS: You'd see everyone.

GRH: That's why crowds frighten me. The crowds in *Waldo*, of course, were terrible, and the crowds in *Slapshot* were terrible. I just have a great horror of them. I don't like the things that happen to people when they get into crowds. My individuals might lose themselves in crowds, but they at least have an entirely different standard to live by. I like individuals, I like individual behavior, I like individual courage.

EFS: In your films, though, the crowd mentality usually seems to come out ahead.

GRH: It does win eventually.

EFS: Is there any hope that individuals can survive?

GRH: Usually not. They're usually tragic figures. Also, they would much rather be with the crowd than be right. It's one of the reasons I was so interested in *Judgment at Nuremburg*, which I directed, was the whole psychology of the German nation and of these people that would be in the concentration camps. They acted like butchers as a group, but as individuals—you get doctors, responsible, ethical people, to suddenly do experiments on Jews because they no longer think that they're human beings. They group-think themselves into the greatest horror that mankind has ever known.

EFS: What Hannah Arendt called the "banality of evil."

GRH: Yes, exactly.

EFS: It seems in some of your films, such as *Slapshot*, you share a similar view, though not quite as jaundiced—

GRH: No, it's fairly jaundiced. The other thing that I think you pointed out was my concern with artists and the number of directors or artists that I've given unflattering portraits to—Peter Sellers as the phony concert pianist, the director in *Waldo Pepper*, the director in *A*

Little Romance, who's an ass. I hate phony artists—that's why I never call myself an artist because I think that the minute you start calling yourself an artist you stop being an artist.

EFS: You seem particularly hard on artists who see themselves as having some sort of message, as carriers of "truth," but are really just playing to an audience.

GRH: I have such contempt for people that do that, and I never want to find myself in that position.

EFS: Will there ever be a "good" artist in your films, one who can successfully communicate with his audience?

GRH: I'm trying to have a good artist in *Garp,* but, of course, he gets shot.

EFS: Not much hope for the artistic fraternity is there?

GRH: [Laughs] No, there isn't.

Notes and References

Editor's Foreword

1. Stuart Byron, *Village Voice*, August 11, 1981, p. 42.

Chapter 1

1. See Gerald Mast, *A Short History of the Movies*, 2d ed. (Indianapolis: Bobbs-Merrill, 1976), pp. 388, 401–2. See also James Monaco, *How to Read a Film* (New York: Oxford University Press, 1977), pp. 261–63.

2. See James Roy MacBean, *Film and Revolution* (Bloomington: Indiana University Press, 1975), pp. 99–103, 312–26.

3. As quoted by Robin Wood, "Religion and Revolution," *Film Comment*, May–June, 1977, pp. 17–23.

4. Mast, *A Short History of the Movies*, pp. 264–65, outlines the conventional morality that ruled Hollywood for thirty years. "In 1934, Joseph Breen went to work for the Motion Pictures Producers and Distributors of America; Breen's special responsibility for the Hays Office was to serve as official arbiter of movie morality. Breen, a Catholic layman, was pushed into the office by the newly formed Catholic Legion of Decency, which advised the faithful to avoid those films that were objectionable either as a whole or in part. Breen *published and enforced a formal moral code* to keep the films from being objectionable. Movies were to avoid brutality (by gangsters and especially the police), they were to avoid depicting any kind of sexual promiscuity (unwedded, extramarital, or perverted), and they were to avoid making any illegal or immoral life seem either possible or pleasant. . . . The Breen code made marriage more a sacred institution than a sexual one; the bedroom (with obligatory twin beds) became more ornate and holy than a cathedral." (My italics.)

Robert Sklar, *Movie-Made America* (New York: Vintage, 1975), points out that "not only did the movies amuse and entertain the nation through its most severe economic and social disorder, holding it together by their capacity to create unifying myths and dreams, but movie culture in the 1930's became a dominant culture for many Americans, providing new values and social ideals to replace shattered old traditions" (p. 161). Sklar claims that the Production

Code of 1930, written by two Catholics, Martin I. Quigley and Daniel A. Lord, operated in the following manner: "The code at least faced up to a fact which previous moral regulators had cloaked in ambiguity: without sex and crime pictures, there wouldn't be enough patrons to sustain a movie business. Granting this, Quigley and Father Lord sought to devise a formula that would keep sex and crime pictures within moral bounds. Their solution allowed for a fairly wide leeway in depicting behavior considered immoral by traditional standards—adultery or murder, for example—so long as some element of 'good' in the story balanced what the code defined as evil. This was the formula of 'compensating moral value': if 'bad' acts are committed, they must be counteracted by punishment and retribution, or reform and regeneration, of the sinful one. 'Evil and good are never to be confused throughout the presentation,' the code said. The guilty must be punished; the audience must not be allowed to sympathize with crime or sin.

"The code went on to prohibit a vast range of human expression and experience—homosexuality, which it described as a 'sex perversion,' interracial sex, abortion, incest, drugs, most forms of profanity . . . and scores of words defined as vulgar" (p. 174).

    5.   Monaco, p. 262.

    6.   Leo Braudy, *The World in a Frame* (Garden City, N.Y.: Anchor Doubleday, 1977), pp. 108, 110.

    7.   *Ibid.*, p. 110.

Chapter 2

    1.   Pauline Kael, "The Bottom of the Pit," *New Yorker*, September 27, 1969, p. 128.

    2.   Vincent Canby, review of *Butch Cassidy and the Sundance Kid*, *New York Times*, September 25, 1969, p. 54, col. 1.

    3.   See "Double Vision," *Time*, September 26, 1969, p. 94. Also Kael, p. 128, tells us that Hill "doesn't really seem to have the style for anything, yet there is a basic decency and intelligence in his work." She also suggests, p. 127, that the film is "a glorified vacuum." Stanley Kauffmann, "On Film," *New Republic*, October 26, 1969, p. 32, tells us that the film is "unfocused and unrealized." Roland Gelatt, "The Old Refrain," *Saturday Review*, September 20, 1969, p. 30, suggests that the film, with its modernisms, is uneven and unsuccessful.

    4.   Kael, p. 128. See also, Henry Hart, review of *Butch Cassidy and the Sundance Kid, Films in Review* 20 (October, 1969):510.

    5.   Kael, pp. 128–29, says that "after watching a put-on rape and Conrad Hall's 'Elvira Madigan' lyric interlude . . . I began to long for something simple and halfway *felt*. If you can't manage genuine sophistication, you may be better off simple." Kauffmann, p. 32, says that "Hill's direction, like the writing, is imitative of everything that's 'in.'" Canby, p. 54, claims that the outlaws' "decline and fall was the sort of alternately absurd and dreamy saga that might have been fantasized by Truffaut's Jules and Jim

and Catherine—before they grew up." John Simon, *Movies into Film* (New York: Delta, 1971), pp. 177–78, finds the film filled with a "plethora of supposedly stylish devices," imitative of *Bonnie and Clyde*, and an attempt to be "very attentive to period flavor, and wildly 'now.'" He claims that "Hill's direction, like Goldman's scenario and Hall's cinematography, is too adorably and calculatedly puckish, as if the film had been made by a bunch of corrupt koalas."

6. Hollis Alpert, "Variations on a Western Theme," *Saturday Review*, September 27, 1969, p. 39.

7. Hart, p. 510.

8. Kael, p. 128.

9. The posse consists of hired guns instead of the traditional group of aroused citizens.

10. All quotes are from the films; any italics have been added.

11. Michael Wood, *America in the Movies* (New York: Basic Books, 1975), pp. 24–51.

12. In the documentary film, *The Making of Butch Cassidy and the Sundance Kid*, Hill remarks that he experimented with foliage masks to screen the actors' faces. The experiment was rejected because it was too awkward, but the remark shows that Hill's use of a screen would not be accidental.

13. The outlaws' inability to cope with the new world is also illustrated by Sundance's remark that he is from New Jersey. He left the East because he could not find a compatible life there.

Chapter 3

1. Typical is Charles Champlin, in a review for the *Los Angeles Times*, March 24, 1972, partially reprinted in "*Slaughterhouse-Five*," *Film Facts* 15, no. 5 (1972):93. Champlin writes that "*Slaughterhouse-Five* is perhaps not intellectually profound, but it is impassioned, warm, human and positive. Its last images are of a blissful nursing mother and happy father in a kind of geodesic heaven with decor by Sears set amidst styrofoam clouds beneath a Rodgers & Hart moon. It's a multi-message which I think can be said to say that the terrestrial and celestial paradise may not be that different; the trick is knowing and appreciating what the earthly treasures are. The power of Vonnegut's work is that he reads all the bad vibes in the world, the horrors, the cruelties, the insanities, but counterattacks with kindness, love, forgiveness and understanding, virtues which grow more fantastic every day."

Other critics who liked the film generally agreed with Champlin's reading. See, for example, Arthur Knight, "Space Craft," *Saturday Review*, April 15, 1972, pp. 10–11; Colin Westerbeck, "The Screen," *Commonweal*, July 28, 1972, pp. 405–6; and Daniel Brudnoy, "Films," *National Review*, August 18, 1972, pp. 911–12.

Those who disliked the film did so because they felt the optimism was muddled or unjustified. For example, Paul Zimmerman, "Pilgrim's Progress," *Newsweek,* April 3, 1972, p. 85; Stephen Farber, "'Slaughterhouse': Return to Shangri-la?" *New York Times,* June 11, 1972, sec. 2, p. 13, col. 1; and Stanley Kauffmann, "On Films," *New Republic,* May 13, 1972, p. 35.

2. Harold Lloyd and Jerry Lewis made careers out of playing just such characters. See Stuart Kaminsky, *American Film Genres* (Dayton, Ohio: Pflaum-Standard, 1976), pp. 160–70.

3. This argument might counter those critics who found the time-tripping uneffective. See Vincent Canby, review of *Slaughterhouse-Five, New York Times,* March 23, 1972, p. 51, col. 1. See also, Penelope Gilliat, "Slaughterhouse," *New Yorker,* April 1, 1972, p. 53.

4. Richard Shickel, "An so it goes—onscreen," *Life,* April 28, 1972, p. 16, suggests "the withdrawals and fantasies . . . are Pilgrim's principal defense against the terrors of the times and finally become his principal reality."

5. Canby, p. 54, col. 1, and Kauffmann, p. 35, both suggest Billy is meant to be "Everyman."

Chapter 4

1. Pauline Kael, review of *The Sting, New Yorker,* December 31, 1973, pp. 49–50.

2. Paul Zimmerman, "The Smiling Monopoly," *Newsweek,* December 17, 1973, p. 92.

3. Stanley Kauffmann, "On Films," *New Republic,* February 2, 1974, p. 20; Colin Westerbeck, "The Screen," *Commonweal,* April 12, 1974, pp. 133–34; John Simon, "Films," *Esquire,* March, 1974, p. 72.

4. Stanley Solomon, *Beyond Formula* (New York: Harcourt, Brace, Jovanovich, 1976), p. 167.

5. Kaminsky, pp. 74–86.

6. Solomon, pp. 168–69.

7. For typical comments on the commercial movie's illusion of integrity, see Allan Casebier, *Film Appreciation* (New York: Harcourt, Brace, Jovanovich, 1976), p. 62, and MacBean, pp. 122–23 and passim.

8. Kaminsky notes the need to make the protagonists sympathetic (p. 69) and that the antagonistic force is almost always monolithic (p. 78). In the typical genre film, the two opposing forces are not joined.

9. Solomon, p. 168, suggests we do not make moral judgments of criminal action directed at other criminals. But, while partially true, the statement is an oversimplification. Although the criminal world may be alien to our own, we continue to make emotional and moral judgments on it, applying our values to the characters and their actions. Circumstances may mitigate our judgments somewhat, but they do not alter them. A crime such as murder remains a crime unless there are significant ameliorating circumstances, such as self-defense.

10. Solomon, p. 169.

Chapter 5

1. See Stanley Kauffmann, "Rubinstein, Redford, and Bolkan," *New Republic*, March 22, 1975, pp. 22, 33; Pauline Kael, "Rear Guard," *New Yorker*, March 24, 1975, pp. 94–99; Michael Buckley, review of *The Great Waldo Pepper*, *Films in Review*, 26, no. 4 (August, 1975): 245–46; Paul Zimmerman, "Outside Loop," *Newsweek*, March 17, 1975, p. 93; Richard Shickel, "High Flying," *Time*, March 24, 1975, p. 9, was one of the minority that liked the film.

2. As Kael says, "the boy is blond and old-movie freckled, and he's going to grow up to be just like Waldo, whom he idolizes; we know we're meant to think that boy is Waldo as he once was"(p. 97).

Chapter 6

1. Books on the darker side of sports range from exposes such as Jim Bouton's *Ball Four* (New York: World, 1970), Dave Meggysey's *Out Of Their League* (Berkeley: Ramparts, 1970), and Gary Shaw's *Meat on the Hoof* (New York: St. Martin's, 1972) to more studied considerations such as Robert Lipsyte's *SportsWorld* (New York: Times Books, 1975) and Neil D. Isaac's *Jock Culture U.S.A.* (New York: Norton, 1978).

Chapter 7

1. Critical reviews of the film were mixed. Most of the negative reviews were similar to that of David Denby, "Little Boy Meets Little Girl," *New York*, May 14, 1979, p. 80. He found the film too calculated, commercial, and timid to be successful. Those who liked the film found it an entertaining, traditional movie. David Ansen, "Puppy Love in the Afternoon," *Newsweek*, April 30, 1979, p. 81, is typical, noting the film's "conscious evocation of 'Romeo and Juliet'," and finding it "a sophisticated fable about innocence and romantic heroism battling to survive in a world that won't long tolerate such grand illusion."

2. The scene of Daniel stealing a movie poster is an allusion to a similar scene in Francois Truffaut's *The 400 Blows*, another film about a confused adolescent.

Selected Bibliography

1. Books

Fenin, George N., and Everson, William K. *The Western*. New York: Grossman, 1973. Brief description of *Butch Cassidy* as a revisionist Western, pp. 362–63.

Solomon, Stanley. *Beyond Formula*. New York: Harcourt, Brace, Jovanovich, 1976. Discusses *Butch Cassidy* and *The Sting* as examples of their respective genres, pp. 55–58, 167–69.

Wright, Will. *Six Guns and Society*. Berkeley: University of California Press, 1975. A study of the Western using a structuralist approach. *Butch Cassidy and the Sundance Kid* is one of five films used to build the structural model. References on pp. 85, 95, 98ff., 168, 169, 172, 173.

2. Articles

Appelbaum, Ralph. "Flying High." *Films and Filming* 25, no. 11 (August, 1979): 10–17. A long interview with Hill about the filming of *A Little Romance* in particular and his films in general.

Atwell, L. "Two Studies in Space-Time." *Film Quarterly* 26, no. 2 (Winter, 1972–73):2–9. Discusses movement in films through space and time in relation to *Je t'aime, Je t'aime* and *Slaughterhouse-Five*.

Comerford, Adelaide. "Period of Adjustment." *Films in Review*, 13 (December, 1962):627.

Crowdus, Gary. "*Butch Cassidy and the Sundance Kid*." *Film Society Review*, March, 1970, pp. 33–37.

Davidson, Bill. "The Entertainer." *New York Times Magazine*, March 16, 1975, pp. 18, 68–70, 76. An extended personality piece on Hill. One of the few interviews he has given.

Davies, Brenda. "*Period of Adjustment*." *Sight and Sound* 32, no. 2 (Spring, 1963):93.

Dimeo, Stephen. "Reconciliation: *Slaughterhouse-Five*, The Film and Novel." *Film Heritage* 8 no. 2 (Winter, 1972–73):1–12. Discusses similarities and differences between the film and the novel.

Eyles, Allen. "*The World of Henry Orient*." *Films and Filming* 10, no. 10 (July, 1964), 20–21.

Farber, Stephen. "*Slaughterhouse*: Return to Shangri-la." *New York Times,* June 11, 1972, sec. 2, p. 13, col. 1. A review which categorizes the film as a syrupy, wrongheaded effort. Farber finds no ironic bite to mitigate against the retreat from reality expressed in Billy's philosophy.

————. "The Spectacle Film: 1967." *Film Quarterly* 20 (Summer, 1967):11–15. A discussion of five spectacle films, including *Hawaii.* Discusses both the film's merits, including its depiction of American expansionism, and its flaws, such as the unevenness of the script and the meaningful use of the epic elements.

————. "*Thoroughly Modern Millie.*" *Film Quarterly* 21, no. 1 (Fall, 1967):62.

Feeney, F. X. "The Sting." In *Magill's Survey of Cinema: English Language Films,* edited by Frank N. Magill. Englewood Cliffs, N.J.: Salem Press, 1980, pp. 1634–37.

Gow, Gordon. "*Toys in the Attic.*" *Films and Filming* 10, no. 3 (December, 1963):38.

Hampton, Charles. "*Butch Cassidy and the Sundance Kid.*" *Film Comment* 6, no. 3 (Fall, 1970):64–69.

Hart, Henry. "*Butch Cassidy and the Sundance Kid.*" *Films in Review* 20, no. 8 (October, 1969): 510–11.

Hunt, Dennis. "*Butch Cassidy and the Sundance Kid.*" *Film Quarterly* 23, no. 2 (Winter, 1969–70):62–63.

Isaacs, N. D. "Unstuck in Time: *Clockwork Orange* and *Slaughterhouse-Five.*" *Literature/Film Quarterly* 1, no. 2 (1973):122–31.

Milne, Tom. "*Butch Cassidy and the Sundance Kid.*" *Sight and Sound* 39, no. 2 (Spring, 1970):101–2.

Nelson, Joyce. "*Slaughterhouse-Five*: Novel and Film." *Literature/Film Quarterly* 1, no. 2 (1973):149–53.

Rothschild, Elaine. "*The World of Henry Orient.*" *Films in Review* 15, no. 4 (April, 1964):242–43.

Sarne, Michael. "*Hawaii.*" *Films and Filming* 13, no. 6 (March, 1967):30–31.

Sarris, Andrew. "*The World of Henry Orient.*" *Village Voice* June 11, 1964, p. 13.

————. "*Thoroughly Modern Millie.*" *Village Voice,* June 22, 1967, p. 21.

Sharples, Win. "The Art of Filmmaking: An Analysis of *Slaughterhouse-Five.*" *Filmmakers Newsletter* 6, no. 1 (November, 1972):24–28. Contains a good discussion of Dede Allen's editing.

Sturhahn, Lawrence. "The Big Con." *North American Review* 259, no. 3 (Fall, 1974):76–80. Considers the sociological implications of *The Sting.*

Thomas, Bob. "Award Winner." *Action* 9, no. 3 (May–June, 1974):29–32. Hill discusses *The Sting* plus his early career in television and theater.

Young, Vernon. "Nobody Lives Here Any More." *Hudson Review* 29, no. 2 (Summer, 1976):263–64. Contains a brief appreciation of *The Great Waldo Pepper.*

Filmography

PERIOD OF ADJUSTMENT (Metro-Goldwyn-Mayer, 1962)
Producer: Lawrence Weingarten
Assistant Director: Al Jennings
Screenplay: Isobel Lennart, from Tennessee Williams's play, *A Period of Adjustment* (1960)
Director of Photography: Paul C. Vogel
Art Directors: George W. Davis, Edward Carfagno
Set Decoration: Henry Grace, Dick Pefferle
Music: Lyn Murray
Recording Supervisor: Franklin Milton
Film Editor: Frederic Steinkamp
Cast: Tony Franciosa (Ralph Baitz), Jane Fonda (Isabel Haverstick), Jim Hutton (George Haverstick), Lois Nettleton (Dorothea Baitz), John McGiver (Stewart P. McGill)
Running Time: 112 minutes, black and white
Premiere: October, 1962
16mm rental: Films, Inc.

TOYS IN THE ATTIC (United Artists, 1963)
Producer: Walter Mirisch
Assistant Director: Emmett Emerson
Screenplay: James Poe, from Lillian Hellman's play, *Toys in the Attic* (1960)
Director of Photography: Joseph Biroc
Art Director: Cary Odell
Set Decoration: Victor Gangelin
Costumes: Bill Thomas
Music: George Duning
Film Editors: Stuart Gilmore, Marshall M. Borden
Cast: Dean Martin (Julian Berniers), Geraldine Page (Carrie Berniers), Yvette Mimieux (Lily Prine Berniers), Wendy Hiller (Anna Berniers), Gene Tierney (Albertine Prine)
Running Time: 90 minutes, black and white
Premiere: June 17, 1963, New Orleans
16mm rental: United Artists 16

THE WORLD OF HENRY ORIENT (United Artists, 1964)
Producer: Jerome Hellman
Assistant Directors: Michael Hertzberg, Roger Rothstein
Screenplay: Nora Johnson, Nunnally Johnson, from Nora Johnson's novel
  The World of Henry Orient (1958)
Director of Photography: Boris Kaufman, Arthur J. Ornitz
Production Design: James Sullivan
Art Director: Jan Scott
Set Decoration: Kenneth Krausgill
Costumes: Ann Roth
Music: Elmer Bernstein; theme "Henry Orient Concerto" by Ken Lauber
Film Editor: Stuart Gilmore
Sound Mix: Robert Martin
Cast: Peter Sellers (Henry Orient), Paula Prentiss (Stella), Tippy Walker
  (Valerie Boyd), Merrie Spaeth (Marian Gilbert), Angela Lansbury (Isabel
  Boyd), Tom Bosley (Frank Boyd), Phyllis Thaxter (Mrs. Gilbert)
Running Time: 106 minutes
Premiere: March 19, 1964, New York
16mm rental: United Artists 16

HAWAII (United Artists, 1966)
Producer: Walter Mirisch
Associate Producer: Lewis J. Rachmil
Assistant Director: Ray Gosnell
Second Unit Director: Richard Talmadge
Prologue Sequence Supervision: James Blue, Daniel Vandraegen
Screenplay: Dalton Trumbo, Daniel Taradash, from James A. Michener's
  novel *Hawaii* (1959)
Director of Photography: Russell Harlan
Second Unit Camera: Harold Wellman
Prologue Sequence Camera: Charles Wheeler
Production Design: Cary Odell
Art Director: James Sullivan
Set Decoration: Edward G. Boyle, Raymond G. Boltz
Costume Design: Dorothy Jeakins
Music: Elmer Bernstein
Sound: Robert Martin, Bert Hallberg
Sound Editor: Wayne Fury
Choreography: Miriam Nelson
Film Editor: Stuart Gilmore
Visual Effects Editor: Marshall M. Borden
Special Photographic Effects: Film Effects of Hollywood, Linwood Dunn,
  James Gordon
Cast: Julie Andrews (Jerusha Bromley), Max von Sydow (Abner Hale),
  Richard Harris (Rafer Hoxworth), Carroll O'Connor (Charles Bromley),

Jocelyne La Garde (Malama), Manu Tupou (Keoki), Ted Nobriga (Kelolo), Elizabeth Logue (Noelani)
Running Time: 189 minutes
Premiere: October 10, 1966
16mm rental: United Artists 16; Macmillan-Audio Brandon
Note: Fred Zinneman withdrew as director before shooting began; Hill was fired during production, but after being temporarily replaced by Arthur Hiller, returned to finish the film.

THOROUGHLY MODERN MILLIE (Universal Pictures, 1967)

Producer: Ross Hunter
Assistant Directors: Douglas Green, John Anderson, Jr., Joe Boston, Phil Parslow
Screenplay: Richard Morris
Director of Photography: Russell Metty (additional photography by Russell Harlan, who temporarily replaced Metty during production)
Art Directors: Alexander Golitzen, George C. Webb
Set Decoration: Howard Bristol
Gowns Design: Jean Louis
Music: Elmer Bernstein; musical numbers scored by Andre Previn; musical supervision, Joseph Gershenson
Songs: *"Thoroughly Modern Millie," "The Tapioca," "The Tap-Tap-Tapioca"* by Sammy Cahn and James Van Huesen; *"The Jewish Wedding Song"* *("Trinkt le Chaim")* by Sylvia Neufeld; *"Jimmy"* by Jay Thompson; *"Poor Butterfly"* by Ray Hubbell and John Golden; *"Do It Again"* by George Gershwin and Bud G. De Sylva; *"Stumblin"* by Zez Confrey; *"The Japanese Sandman"* by Richard A. Whiting and Raymond B. Egan; and *"Rose of Washington Square"* by Ballard McDonald and James F. Hanley.
Sound: Waldon O. Watson, William Russell, Ronald Pierce, Don Cunliffe, Perry Devore, Bruce Smith
Film Editor: Stuart Gilmore
Assistant Editor: Richard Bracken
Cast: Julie Andrews (Millie Dillmount), Mary Tyler Moore (Dorothy Brown), Carol Channing (Muzzy Van Hossmere), James Fox (Jimmy Smith), Beatrice Lillie (Mrs. Meers), John Gavin (Trevor Graydon)
Running Time: 138 minutes, color
Premiere: March 21, 1967
16mm rental: Macmillan-Audio Brandon; Swank (St. Louis); Twyman
Note: Elmer Bernstein won an Academy Award for best original music score

BUTCH CASSIDY AND THE SUNDANCE KID (Twentieth Century-Fox, 1969)

Producer: John Foreman
Executive Producer: Paul Monash
Assistant Director: Steven Bernhardt
Second Unit Director: Michael Moore

Screenplay: William Goldman
Director of Photography: Conrad Hall
Second Unit Photography: Harold E. Wellman
Art Directors: Jack Martin Smith, Phillip Jeffries
Set Decoration: Walter M. Scott, Chester L. Bayhi
Costumes: Edith Head
Music: Burt Bacharach
Sound: William E. Edmondson, David Dockendorf
Film Editors: John C. Howard, Richard C. Meyer
Cast: Paul Newman (Butch Cassidy), Robert Redford (The Sundance Kid), Katharine Ross (Etta Place), Strother Martin (Percy Garris), George Furth (Woodcock)
Running Time: 110 minutes
Premiere: September 23, 1969, New Haven, Connecticut
16mm rental: Films, Inc.
Note: William Goldman won an Academy Award for best screenplay; Conrad Hall for cinematography; and Burt Bacharach for best original score. The song *"Raindrops Keep Fallin' on My Head"* by Bacharach and Hal David won the Academy Award for best song. Sung by B. J. Thomas

SLAUGHTERHOUSE-FIVE (A Universal-Vanadas Picture, 1972)
Producer: Paul Monash
Executive Producer: Jennings Lang
Screenplay: Stephen Geller, from the novel *Slaughterhouse-Five or the Children's Crusade*, by Kurt Vonnegut, Jr.
Assistant Director: Ray Gosnell
Director of Photography: Miroslav Ondricek. Special photographic consultant, Enzo Martinelli
Production Design: Henry Bumstead
Art Directors: Alexander Golitzen and George Webb
Set Decorations: John McCarthy
Music: Glenn Gould, adapted from the works of Johann Sebastian Bach
Sound: Milan Novotny, James Alexander, and Richard Vorisek
Film Editor: Dede Allen
Cast: Michael Sacks (Billy Pilgrim), Ron Leibman (Paul Lazzaro), Valerie Perrine (Montana Wildhack), Eugene Roche (Edward Derby), Sharon Gans (Valencia)
Premiere: March, 1972
Running Time: 104 minutes
16mm rental: Swank, Twyman, Clem Williams Films

THE STING (Universal, 1973)
Producers: Tony Bill, Michael and Julia Phillips
Associate Producer: Robert L. Crawford
Assistant Director: Ray Gosnell
Second Assistant Director: Charles Dismukes

Screenplay: David S. Ward
Director of Photography: Robert Surtees
Art Director: Henry Bumstead
Set Decoration: James Payne
Costumes: Edith Head
Music: Martin Hamlisch, adapted from the music of Scott Joplin
Sound: Robert Bertrand and Ronald Pierce
Editor: William Reynolds
Cast: Paul Newman (Henry Gordorff), Robert Redford (Johnny Hooker),
    Robert Shaw (Doyle Lonnegan), Eileen Brennan (Billie), Harold Gould
    (Kid Twist), Robert Earl Jones (Luther Coleman), Charles Dierkop (Floyd)
Running Time: 129 minutes
Premiere: December, 1973
16mm rental: Swank, Twyman, Clem Williams Films
Note: The film won seven Academy Awards, including best director for Hill,
    best picture, screenplay, art direction/set decoration, costumes, editing,
    and music score.

THE GREAT WALDO PEPPER (Universal, 1975)
Producer: George Roy Hill
Associate Producer: Robert L. Crawford
Assistant Director: Ray Gosnell
Screenplay: William Goldman, from a story by George Roy Hill
Director of Photography: Robert Surtees
Art Director: Henry Bumstead
Set Decoration: James Payne
Costumes: Edith Head
Music: Henry Mancini
Sound: Bob Miller and Ronald Pierce
Air Sequences Supervised by: Frank Tallman
Film Editor: William Reynolds
Cast: Robert Redford (Waldo Pepper), Bo Svenson (Alex Olsson), Bo Brun-
    din (Ernst Kessler), Susan Sarandon (Mary Beth), Edward Herrmann
    (Ezra), Philip Bruns (Dillhoefer), Margot Kidder (Maudie)
Running Time: 107 minutes:
Premiere: March, 1975
16mm rental: Swank, Twyman, Clem Williams Films

SLAPSHOT (Universal Pictures, 1977)
Producers: Robert J. Wunsch and Stephan Friedman
Associate Producer: Robert L. Crawford
Assistant Directors: James Westman, Tom Joyner, Wayne Farlow, and Peter
    Burrell
Screenplay: Nancy Dowd

Director of Photography: Victor Kemper
Art Director: Henry Bumstead
Set Decoration: James Payne
Costumes: Tom Bronson
Music: Elmer Bernstein
Sound: Don Sharpless and Peter Berkos
Film Editor: Dede Allen
Cast: Paul Newman (Reggie Dunlop), Michael Ontkean (Ned Braden), Lindsay Crouse (Lily Braden), Jennifer Warren (Francine Dunlop), Andrew Duncan (Jim Carr), Strother Martin (Joe McGrath)
Running Time: 123 minutes
Premiere: February, 1977
16mm rental: Swank Films (St. Louis)

A LITTLE ROMANCE (Orion, 1979)
Producer: Yves Rousset-Rouard and Robert L. Crawford
Executive Producer: Patrick Kelley
Assistant Director: Carlo Lastricati
Second Assistant Director: John Pepper
Screenplay: Allan Burns, from Patrick Cauvin's novel $E = mc^2$, *Mon Amour*
Director of Photography: Pierre William Glenn
Production Design: Henry Bumstead
Art Director: Francois De Lamothe
Set Decoration: Robert Christides
Wardrobe: Rosine Delamare
Sound: Michel Desrois
Film Editor: William Reynolds
Associate Film Editor: Claudine Bouche
Music: Georges Delerue
Cast: Laurence Olivier (Julius), Thelonious Bernard (Daniel), Diane Lane (Lauren), Arthur Hill (Richard King), Sally Kellerman (Kay King), David Dukes (George Di Marco), Broderick Crawford (himself)
Running Time: 108 minutes
Premiere: March, 1979
16mm rental: Films, Inc.

Index